BECOMING HUMAN

Other titles by Warren Bardsley

Touched by Grace:
Walking the Path of Grief
(Published by Church in the Market Place, 2005)

Fair City:
One Community's Fair Trade Campaign
(Published by Church in the Market Place, 2008)

Passion and Power:
Conflict and Change in 7th Century Britain
(Published by Warren Bardsley, 2009)

Letters from Jerusalem:
Reflections of an Ecumenical Accompanier
(Published by Church in the Market Place, 2010)

Dancing
(Published by Church in the Market Place, 2012)

Becoming Human

An appreciation of the life and ministry of Geoffrey Ainger

Warren Bardsley

Best wishes

Warren Bardsley

The glory of God is a human being fully alive
(St. Irenaeus)

CHURCH IN THE MARKET PLACE PUBLICATIONS

2014

Church in the Market Place Publications

Cover design by Morag Burton

British Library Cataloguing in Publication Data
A record for this book is available from the British Library

ISBN 978-1-899147-98-4

Typeset in Baskerville Old Face
by RefineCatch Ltd, Bungay, Suffolk

Printed in Great Britain by
Cambrian Printers, Aberystwyth
Paper from sustainable source/FSC managed

For Barbara, Margaret, Paul, Colin
and their families

Contents

Contents

All these sermons were preached at Orpington
Methodist Church. *Amen* (v) was Geoff's last
sermon before retirement.

Preface

My friendship with Geoff Ainger began when I moved to Lichfield in 2004 following the death of my wife Joan. The week after I arrived, the Aingers invited me to a meal in their home, the first of many! My immediate impression of Geoff was of a big man, yet not intimidating. I sensed a shyness about him, yet a welcoming warmth, and I felt immediately at home.

He said, 'conviviality is at the heart of the gospel'. During these Lichfield years, I have been richly blessed by Geoff and Barbara's friendship and their generous hospitality.

This small book is very much a personal appreciation of Geoff; I have, however, drawn on the memories of a number of people who knew him far longer and much better than myself. I am grateful for their contributions; I have tried to allow their stories to be heard. I am especially grateful to Geoff's widow, Barbara, and to the Rev. Donald Eadie, who have collaborated in this project from the outset and have been involved at every stage of the writing. Barbara made Geoff's papers available to me, tapes of some of his sermons and an interview he gave as part of an Oral History project in Notting Hill. As well as writing an epilogue to this book, Donald has provided valuable information from personal experience of that place and time; equally important are those insights from his friendship with Geoff over a long period. Both Barbara and Donald have made several helpful suggestions and saved me from a number of errors along the way!

My over-riding purpose throughout has been to let Geoff speak and to allow his distinctive voice to be heard. In a conversation some weeks before he died, we talked about the possibility of this book. He made it clear that he would want anything that was written about him to reflect the major themes of his journey and the bedrock convictions which undergirded and nourished his spirituality throughout his life, including the dark wilderness years of his breakdown and beyond. Above all, he wanted to bear witness to the transcendent, transforming power of grace. I have tried to be faithful to that request.

I offer it with a sense of inadequacy but also of gratitude for the enrichment of Geoff's friendship during the all-too-short time that I knew him. It has been a labour of love.

Warren R Bardsley
Lichfield, June 2014

Acknowledgements

The hymns, 'Born in the Night', 'A Cry in the Night', and 'Come Holy Spirit', are reproduced by kind permission of Stainer & Bell, London, England, www.stainer.co.uk

I am grateful for permission to quote from the following publications:

The Other Notting Hill, Chris Holmes, Brewin Press, 2005.
Jacob and the Prodigal, Kenneth E. Bailey, InterVarsity Press USA, 2003.
Holy Listening, Margaret Guenther, DLT, 1993.
Reflections on Exile, Edward W.Said, Granta Books, 2001.
Jesus our Contemporary, Geoff Ainger, SCM Press, 1967.

I have quoted extensively from an article which Geoff wrote in 1977 (A Pilgrimage in Theology), which was published by the Epworth Review in that year, and 'News from Notting Hill' by Mason, Denny and Ainger (1967).

Thanks to Peter and Margaret Daone for their painstaking work in preparing a selection of Geoff's recorded sermons for inclusion on the accompanying CD, and to Colin Atkin for preparing the master copy for reproducction.

As always I am indebted to my friend and publisher Robert Davies for his encouragement and support.

Prologue

Born in the night: a London nativity

For the majority of church-goers, the name of Geoffrey Ainger is inextricably linked with a Christmas carol which he wrote in the late 1950s – although I would hazard a guess that among those who have sung it regularly over the years, most would be unable to name the author. It is undoubtedly one of the finest modern hymns about the birth of Christ having been translated into numerous languages and, after its initial publication by Stainer and Bell, has found its place in a number of denominational and ecumenical collections.

However, fewer still are aware of the story behind the hymn. Geoff was minister in the London suburb of Loughton at the time, having recently returned from the United States where he had combined study for a Master's degree with involvement in the work of the East Harlem Protestant Parish in New York. One Christmas he was asked by his church youth club to write the script for a nativity play. Instead of the traditional format with shepherds and wise men in Middle Eastern dress, Geoff placed the familiar story in a modern setting. A young couple arrive from the north at a nearby railway station late at night. She is heavily pregnant and they begin to look for accommodation in the town, eventually arriving tired and hungry at a local petrol station where the owner's wife finds them a room above the garage. Some of the locals, hearing of this strange arrival, visit them, offering help. Geoff wrote songs to accompany the script of which 'Born in the night' was one; youth club members played the various parts and accompanied the songs on guitars and drums.

In those days, this was a startling innovation, and not universally welcome! For some, however, it was a deeply moving experience of the reality of the Christmas story. A woman from the church who had witnessed the play couldn't get to sleep that night for thinking of Jesus born in a petrol station! It made a deep impression.

Some years ago, a Christmas card depicted a black and white photograph of a modern Middle Eastern refugee family sitting against a wall surrounded by a couple of packing cases containing all their possessions. Underneath is a quote by the poet, Coventry Patmore:

> I have many things to say to you, but you cannot bear them now ... not because they are so unlike your everyday experiences, but because they are so like.

This is what Geoff was trying to convey – the down-to-earthness of God's coming among us. Properly understood, 'Born in the night' contains the major themes of his theology, which will be explored at deeper levels in this book. We discern the vulnerability of a God who comes to us in need, not to dominate but dependent on our hospitality, 'born in a borrowed room'. And there is a hint of exile and alienation in the words, 'a long way from your home'. At the heart of the hymn is the theme of night and of light piercing the darkness inside us; our ultimate trust in the integrity of God is expressed in those daring words, 'prove it is true – go to your cross of wood', inspiring hope in One who is 'coming soon to reign'. But there is no triumphalism here, simply a longing for the Christ of Bethlehem and Nazareth to 'walk in our streets again', Jesus our Contemporary, our elder Brother, one of us, the Christ of every road, Mary's child.

Prologue

1   Born in the night
     Mary's Child
     a long way from your home;
     coming in need
     Mary's Child
     born in a borrowed room

2   Clear shining light
     Mary's Child
     your face lights up our way;
     light of the world
     Mary's Child
     dawn on our darkened day.

3   Truth of our life
     Mary's Child
     you tell us God is good;
     prove it is true
     Mary's Child
     go to your cross of wood.

4   Hope of the world
     Mary's Child
     you're coming soon to reign;
     King of the earth
     Mary's Child
     walk in our streets again.

ONE

Beginnings

It is not just genes that make us who we become, it is our stories too.

(Michael Morpurgo)

Geoff lived in Lichfield for the last 14 years of his life. He was a founder member of the Erasmus Darwin Society, a group of retired professional men and women who meet every month to read papers on theology, philosophy, science and ethics. He gave a paper once, entitled 'Do I exist? Who wants to know?' In a profound exploration of human identity, punctuated by his characteristic wit and memorable turn of phrase, he maintained that, in the end, it is a theological question. Our human being is rooted in the existence of God in whose image we are made. This question of identity pre-occupied Geoff throughout his life. The Psalmist (139) uttered the astounding words 'Before I was formed in the womb – you knew me.' Even before our conception we were a twinkle in the eye of God! But even if we believe this to be true, our human being and formation is bound up with the genes we inherit through our parents and the environment in which we are nurtured and grow up. We cannot be understood in isolation from the places and the people who have shaped us.

A Norfolk childhood

Geoff was born in the Essex village of Mistley in 1925, the youngest of three sons of Ernest and Ethel Ainger. When he was five the family moved to Norwich, capital of the county of

Norfolk, where he was to spend the rest of his childhood and adolescence. His father was stationmaster at Norwich, a prestigious occupation in those days, and, by the standards of the time, the Ainger family was in material terms comfortably off. Norfolk is a rural county with a long coastline to the east, running from Kings Lynn to Great Yarmouth and with fenland on its western boundary. Local character traits are shaped as much by geography as by history and the sturdy independence and reserve of the Norfolk people may stem, partly at least, from (until recent times) its relative isolation.

My own arrival in the county as a probationer minister in 1962 was something of a culture shock, having lived all my life in industrial Lancashire. It was a different world and there were numerous times during the first few weeks when I got lost along the narrow, winding country lanes! Prior to our arrival, some wiseacre told my wife and I that the county motto was 'do different' and that the locals were very difficult to get to know. We found this to be far from the case. I look back on that time with real affection, on friendships made, and important lessons learned. Two of my Norfolk heroes are Robert Kett and Julian of Norwich. Kett of Wymondham was a yeoman farmer who led a 16th-century rebellion in the county against the injustice of enclosure by wealthy landowners; Mother Julian, the 14th-century anchoress, widely regarded as one of the greatest mystics of all time, whose writings on divine love have inspired millions. Two complementary sides of the coin of authentic Christian spirituality; a passion for justice rooted in the life of prayer, which was to some extent reflected in the Primitive Methodist, nonconformist tradition in which Geoff was nurtured.

He wrote affectionately of his upbringing in that environment.

I was lucky enough to grow up in a devout and thoroughly humane Methodist family, in a good, very normal congregation in Norwich. I still remember from those days, the 'financial thermometers' fixed up on the organ pipes, telling us how much we had to raise by the end of the year; the Good Friday teas and cantatas, and the old men who used to shout 'Hallelujah! Amen!' in praise of God and for the distraction of small boys during eternal sermons! I remember the regular evangelical missions – and my own seven or eight 'conversions' in response to 'the invitation'! I look back with gratitude to that community, to its routine faithfulness, its capacity for humour and moments of authentic inspiration. However naively and spasmodically, my theological journey, such as it has been, has its conscious beginnings in that experience.

Calling

Strangely, it was not in the chapel but in a cinema that Geoff believed he had been addressed by the voice of God. Like many teenagers of his day, he went regularly to the 'pictures' on a Saturday night. On this particular occasion, the film showing was 'Stanley and Livingstone' with Spencer Tracey; it dramatized Stanley's epic trek into the interior of Africa to find Livingstone at Ujiji. He recalled, 'When I left the cinema I was convinced that God had called me to the ministry,' though the deeper significance of that experience didn't become clear to him until much later, during a dark period of his life.

Scott Memorial Methodist Church in Thorpe (now an insurance office!) was Geoff's home chapel. Here, he shared in the leadership of worship with the youth fellowship, eventually became a local preacher and, together with several other young people (some of them local preachers), was part of the 'Larkman Group', initiated by another preacher, the Rev.

Norwyn Denny who later became chairman of the Liverpool District and President of Conference. He and Geoff shared a deep, lifelong friendship and were colleagues in the Notting Hill Group Ministry in the 1960s. The Larkman Group fostered innovative, often open-air, work on the Larkman estate in Earlham and eventually at various other places around Norwich. Other members of the group included the Rev John Hastings and Dennis Frary, who is still active in a neighbouring circuit. Others are now scattered across the country, all with a wider vision of the gospel nurtured in this early experience.

By the time he left school, the war in Europe was entering its fifth year. He had been turned down for military service on health grounds, but at the age of nineteen, as the final Allied advance through France to Germany began, Geoff found himself working with the Church Army serving meals to troops from mobile canteens. Europe was in ruins; everywhere was devastation and despair. Millions had been slaughtered or maimed during the six-year conflict. Out of the ashes of war and the struggle for domination between east and west, a new Europe would eventually emerge. For the young Geoff Ainger, his first contact with the continent was salutary; it marked the beginnings of an encounter that was to be a major influence on his theological and political development.

TWO

Formation

One does not discover new lands without consenting to lose sight of the shore.

(André Gide)

After the war it was several years before life returned to any kind of normality and future plans had to be put on hold. Although Geoff was still determined to candidate for the Methodist ministry, colleges remained closed with training temporarily suspended.

So for the next two years, he took up an appointment in the Lowestoft circuit as a lay worker, visiting the scattered villages on his bike, taking services and meetings. In 1948 his candidacy was accepted, and under normal circumstances training would have commenced the following September at one of Methodism's six theological colleges. However, such was the shortage of ministers in 1948 that Geoff was sent to Motherwell in Scotland as a 'pre-collegiate' candidate, which he described as 'somewhat akin to the experience of being led like a lamb to the slaughter'!

Training for ministry

It is worth mentioning at this point how much ministerial formation has changed over the years. When Geoff entered Richmond College in 1950 the emphasis was on academic theology and the expectation was that, if qualified, students would be placed on a degree course. Describing his years at Richmond he said, we were taken in hand by highly competent 'couriers' who could lead us on journeys ... into unexplored territories of the Old and New Testaments and of church history, with a few 'day excursions' to the nearer shores of psychology, pastoral theology, ethics and the like. I am grateful for this thorough and painstaking grounding in biblical studies ... but, on recollection, most of our theology seems to have been done in the past tense. When I left, I felt better acquainted with the early church fathers than with such contemporary thinkers as Barth, Brunner, Niebhur, Tillich and Büber.

Generally speaking, that would have been the experience of most students in that era. The changes of the past half-century have reflected both fresh educational insights into how people learn, plus recognition of the importance of practical experience alongside academic discipline and the dynamic interaction between both.

New horizons

Geoff's first real experience of the Ecumenical Movement came at the end of his time at Richmond. Significantly, it was to be in Europe. He spent three weeks at the Ecumenical Institute in Bossé, Switzerland. During that time he visited the Taizé Community and talked with Catholic worker priests in Paris.

Open-ness to the world and serious Bible study which characterized those communities made a deep impression on me and impacted on my subsequent ministry out of all proportion to the length of time I spent among those people. It was at this time, too, that I really discovered Dietrich Bonhoeffer, whose 'Letters and Papers from prison' became for me what they have been for so many others, basic reading in theological perception and spiritual discernment.

Seeds were being sown, one of which was Geoff's growing conviction of the crucial importance of collaborative, or group ministry for the future of the church.

This seed began to germinate during his first circuit appointment at Totton, a district of Southampton where he was ordained and married to Lois in the same year. It was during this period that he became a founder member of a small group of young ministers who were deeply concerned about the future of the church. They met in Birmingham around the question, 'Do we need some kind of group to enable ministers of our era, who share similar concerns, to be supportive to each other?' The group had much in common: all were graduates, had worked in ecumenical fields, were passionate about Methodism and serious about theology. Some time later, a larger group of around 25 was convened and, in that meeting, the 'Renewal Group' was born.

It was around this time that the name of Bruce Kenrick began to appear on Geoff's horizon and in conversations of the Renewal Group. Bruce, a Scottish minister in the United Reformed Church had gone in the 1950s to the United States to work in the Protestant Parish of East Harlem in New York. He was a charismatic personality whose commitment to social activism was rooted in a radical prophetic theology. East Harlem was an inner city area in New York in which a team of ministers and lay workers had created a new kind of congregation 'characterized by profound commitment to the desperate poverty of the area, earnest protest to politicians, and sacramental worship rooted in the experience of the local community'. Kenrick was to publish a book, *Come Out the*

Wilderness,[1] a vivid account of the work of the parish which influenced a generation of ministers. He was to become an influential figure in later developments at Notting Hill.

Having met Geoff and knowing of his interest in the development of team ministry, Kenrick wrote to him, outlining the project and suggesting that he give serious thought to spending some time in East Harlem. Consequently, during his last year at Southampton he applied to the Methodist Conference for permission to spend a year with the parish, which was granted, and in August 1956 he and Lois sailed for America.

East Harlem

Of this period, Geoff wrote,

> It was in East Harlem that I first came to understand the Church primarily as a 'hearing' community. The Methodism in which I had grown up had been very strong on the 'blessed assurance' of the glorious good news, and very much preoccupied with the problem of communication. 'How to get it across' was the absorbing issue. On the streets of the extraordinarily broken community of East Harlem, and meeting for worship in little storefront centres, I came to realise that the preacher does not have the Word printed, easy of access in his pocket. It is a *spoken* word uttered by the Living God in and through the events of every day. Nor does the word descend to us in vertical purity, straight down to the study or pulpit, 'untouched by human hand'! It is spoken in and through the life and death of the people among whom we live. Not just the good people or 'the examples to us all', but more especially through the puzzled, the failures, the

---

[1] Bruce Kenrick, *Come Out the Wilderness*, Fontana/Collins, 1965.

broken and bewildered. I made the discovery that, in a very real sense my sermons . . . had to be received as a gift from God, through the community before they could be offered back as any kind of living word.

Although Geoff had only applied for permission to serve the Protestant Parish for one year, the opportunity came to spend a second year, studying for a Master's degree at Union Theological seminary under such giants as Reinhold Niebuhr. The British Conference agreed to an extension so, while commuting to Union, he continued to live in the parish and preach on Sundays. This second year was of immense value; involvement with the broken humanity of East Harlem and his theological studies went in tandem, an experience which was to prove highly significant for his future role in Notting Hill. His dissertation focussed on the life and writings of the French Algerian philosopher and novelist, Albert Camus, whose exploration of the human condition in terms of alienation and the apparent futility and absurdity of life made a profound impression on Geoff. In a paper presented to the Darwin Society in 2009 (Albert Camus: *Absurdly Human*), Geoff said,

I am . . . grateful to Camus for his recognition that freedom cannot mean life without limits. In our age of astonishing scientific and technological achievement we need to shift the debate about Eden away from the fanciful chronology of Archbishop Ussher towards a new consideration of the meaning of contingency and responsibility for a truly human life. We can only applaud Camus' acceptance of the invitation to 'live and create in the very midst of the desert'. But I cannot forget that when Jeremiah speaks of his people's liberation from slavery and return from exile he speaks not of defiant creativity in the midst of a deadly environment. He speaks of *grace*.

'Thus, says the Lord: The people who survived the sword found grace in the wilderness.'

Long before Geoff wrote those words, they had become the expression of a deeply traumatic but ultimately liberating phase of his journey that will be explored in later chapters.

Geoff and Lois returned to Britain in 1958, to take up an appointment in the London suburb of Loughton in the Wanstead and Woodford circuit, where two of their three children, Margaret and David, were born. It was, however, events unfolding in another part of London that were destined to significantly change their lives and bring to birth the vision of a radical, prophetic group ministry based on the pattern of East Harlem.

THREE

Notting Hill

Notting Hill in the 1960s was an area of very severe deprivation.

(Chris Holmes)

Mention the name 'Notting Hill' today and most people will think immediately of Julia Roberts, Hugh Grant and the film of that name in which they starred. Chris Holmes (a former Director of the charity, Shelter) in his book, *The Other Notting Hill*, writes:

> The popularity of the film 'Notting Hill' has given the area a world-wide image as a glamorous, exciting area in which to live. Notting Hill in the 1960s was a very different place. It was home to residents with a huge range of incomes and backgrounds; a minority were well-off but *most were poor*.[2]

Social crisis

To understand the origins of the Methodist experiment in group ministry, it is necessary to try to appreciate the huge social changes that were then taking place in that part of West London in the 1950s and 1960s. At the heart of the problem was an acute housing crisis, affecting the whole country, but most severe in the inner-city areas of major conurbations. During the war almost a half-million homes had been destroyed by bombing

---

[2] Chris Holmes, *The Other Notting Hill*, Brewin Books, 2005.

and another half-million were severely damaged. A major house-building programme was launched to replace the old slums with new housing estates, with more than half the homes being built by local authorities. The trouble was that, as those tenants from the cleared areas were given priority, fewer applicants from the local authority waiting list could be re-housed. As sharing and overcrowding became worse in neighbourhoods not covered by the clearance programmes, so did the prospect of being re-housed by the council. It was a vicious circle.

The problem was exacerbated by two other factors. One was the arrival during the 1950s of large numbers of immigrants from the Commonwealth, notably from the West Indies, who had come to London and other large industrial cities in the country, attracted by advertisements for jobs such as those in transport – on the buses and the underground. Hospitals near and far recruited immigrant nurses.

West London, and other areas with their large stock of rundown properties, became a magnet for those seeking places to live. Notting Hill was one of these areas, having the added advantage of being within easy travelling distance of recruiting centres for London Transport, British Rail and the Post Office.

The other factor was the passing of the 1957 Rent Act, which ended controls on new lettings by private landlords. This meant that effectively there were no limits to rents landlords could charge and, for tenants, no security against eviction. Peter Rachman, who gained notoriety during the Profumo–Keeler scandal, was one of those landlords. Rachmanism became a byword for corruption, greed, and the near-unbearable misery inflicted on tenants in run-down, multi-occupied properties. The worst landlords were those who actually hired thugs who were sent round to threaten tenants who complained about repairs or fell behind with their rents. Many tenants lived in a state of constant fear of eviction.

Racial tensions

Those West Indians who came to Notting Hill could not have anticipated the racial discrimination they would face, or the dreadful housing conditions that were experienced by black and white residents alike. Tensions were rising during the late 1950s, encouraged by fascist groups seeking to fan the flames of racial hostility. In 1958 the lid blew off. There were riots in the streets. The flashpoint was the stabbing to death of a black man, Kelso Cochrane, by a group of white men on a street in the heart of North Kensington which had become a powder keg of physical explosiveness and fear.

Although this murder did not become as notorious or as iconic as that of Stephen Lawrence 30 years later, its effect was profound and far-reaching. Mike Phillips, a black writer, in a graphic account of the funeral procession for Kelso Cochrane, wrote,

> ... this was a unique Caribbean occasion, one of the biggest funerals ever seen in North Kensington. About 1,200 people were walking in the procession and more of them lining the streets on the way to Kensal Green cemetery. The man they were burying wasn't someone most of them knew when he was alive. He was a thirty-three year old Jamaican carpenter, born for obscurity ... except that one night in May he had been stabbed to death by a group of whites out for blood. In between the night of his bleeding to death on the pavement and the morning of the service at St Michaels Church in Ladbroke Grove he had become a martyr. West Indians and their supporters were making the ceremony a state funeral, a demonstration which would leave an indelible mark on

the area and its people, and speak to everyone who saw it about their identity and their determination to stay put.[3]

The Church responds

Ironically, the demand for a new Christian initiative in response to this crisis came not from a churchgoer but from an agnostic, a junior Labour Whip on the London County Council, Donald Chesworth. He had persuaded Dr Donald (later Lord) Soper to serve as an Alderman of the London County Council, and had brought home to the former President of the Methodist Conference the desperate needs of the area. On 8th July 1959, at the Bristol Conference, during a discussion following the report on London Mission Affairs Soper intervened, making a powerful case for a radical new approach to the needs of deprived inner-city neighbourhoods where the Church too often seemed almost invisible. In particular he called for a long-term commitment of resources to a community-based approach to mission in Notting Hill and North Kensington. The Conference gave broad consent to the proposal and suggested that consultations be held by Donald Soper and Dr Irvonwy Morgan (chair of the London Mission committee) together with the chairmen of the Methodist districts concerned, with a view to bringing a report in due course. In practice the precise details were left to a small committee of four to work out.

Soper's dramatic intervention at the Bristol Conference had challenged the church to 'do something', but what? It was at this point that an answer came in the form of a memorandum sent to him from three Methodist ministers, David Mason, Norwyn Denny and Geoff Ainger, the fruit of 12 months of hard thinking on the mission of the church in places like Notting Hill. It is extremely important to understand that the suggestions

[3] Quoted in Chris Holmes, *The Other Notting Hill*, Brewin Books, 2005.

contained in this memo were rooted not only in a deep concern for the needs of inner-city areas and an understanding of their underlying causes but for a 'renewal of our understanding of the *theological meaning* of all that we do'. The memorandum's five points stressed the need for a Group Ministry of (initially) ministers and their wives 'bound by common disciplines of prayer, vocation and study ... as a missionary or apostolic community in the life of the world'. They would not seek to be a kind of 'clerical elite'; on the contrary, their task would be to build the congregation and create community.

Group Ministry: a radical experiment

Donald Soper was enthusiastic, and made immediate arrangements to meet the ministers to discuss their proposals. Further sessions followed and eventually a basic structure was agreed, aimed at enabling the birth of a new experimental approach in which the Group Ministry would be central, although the precise details, at that stage, were unclear. The formation of the Notting Hill Group Ministry was a gradual process and was not without its teething troubles. It would, in fact, take over two years for the vision to become reality.

One of the early points of difference concerned location and buildings. Initially, Soper felt that new-build premises were the answer, whereas the three ministers thought otherwise. They were convinced of the importance of beginning with what was already there in terms of buildings and people. Eventually it was agreed that the Lancaster Road and Denbigh Road Methodist Churches would transfer to the West London Mission and become the focal point of the experimental ministry. This was the first step in the formation of the Group Ministry but it was the best part of three years before the group was complete. In order for it to be a smooth transition the support of the local church and circuit was imperative. It was fortunate that the superintendent of the circuit, the Rev. Eric Elliott, who had been in pastoral charge of the Lancaster Road congregation during the previous eight years saw this project as the culmination of his own work and ministry. In the words of David Mason, 'he urged acceptance of the scheme and his enthusiasm and support underwrote all that was being advocated'.[4]

So what happened next?

The ideal would have been for all members of the proposed Group Ministry to move into the area at the same time. However, for practical reasons this was impossible. Although the West London Mission was committed to the experimental project in North Kensington, there was the small but important matter of money! An added complication was that two members of the proposed team were, for the immediate future, formally committed to existing circuit appointments. In the event, the group formed gradually, moving in at yearly intervals, beginning with David and Ann Mason (1960), Norwyn and Ellen Denny (1961), and Geoff and Lois Ainger in 1962. Initially they occupied three different flats in the same house, 19 Blenheim Crescent, later moving into separate manses. This was not an automatic or inevitable progression. The ministers had to argue their case. David Mason had ten years' experience of mission in English cities with a background in social work; and Norwyn Denny had served in Jamaica, having direct experience of the West Indian immigrants who formed a significant part of the area's population. This obvious advantage was strengthened when a Trust connected to the Methodist Missionary Society offered an annual grant of £600 towards Norwyn's stipend.

[4] David Mason, Norwyn Denny and Geoffrey Ainger, *News from Notting Hill: The formation of a group ministry*, Epworth, 1967, p. 12.

The case for a third minister was more difficult to make, yet the Group were convinced of its necessity. This was a pioneer experiment in an inner-city area, suffering multiple social deprivation exacerbated by racial tensions and with the potential for further violent unrest. The argument for Geoff's appointment – that he was literally the only Methodist minister in the country with first-hand experience of a similar Group Ministry – became unanswerable once the case for such a ministry had been won. David Mason said, 'Geoff Ainger would supply the ideas and background, necessary to ensure that Notting Hill became an experiment, and did not stop short of real creative achievement'.[5] So, in 1962, Geoff's name appeared in the first draft of 'stations' as being appointed to the West London Mission and Conference confirmed the arrangement. *The Group Ministry had begun.* Ahead, lay several demanding, exciting, ground-breaking years, which would in significant ways change not only the face of that community but the lives of those who had committed to it.

It might be useful to explain here how this experiment in Group Ministry differed from the traditional Methodist circuit system. This broadly operates on the basis of a team of ministers having pastoral oversight of a number of congregations who, with lay colleagues, seek to work together in terms of policy within the circuit area, which may vary in size, geographically. Ministers appointed to such circuits normally have little or no prior knowledge of each other, may differ widely in personality and background – and, more importantly, in theological conviction and churchmanship.

The three ministers who formed the initial Group Ministry knew each other well. David and Geoff were in Richmond College together and, as previously mentioned, Norwyn and

---

[5] *News from Notting Hill: The formation of a group ministry*, p. 13.

Geoff had been friends for many years. All three were members of the Renewal Group; their theological convictions and their understanding of the mission of the church were similar. And as we have already noted, they had *together* devised a model for the Group Ministry, the outlines of which were clear. It had to be located in a clearly defined area, driven by a rationale rooted in an incarnational theology that took seriously the role of the church in its locality, not only in terms of personal conversion but social transformation. Three outstanding ministers, different in personality but united in purpose and, in the gifts they brought to the Group, complementing one another.

Of course, although the Group Ministry of necessity began with male ministers, it was never intended to be a clerical élite or a bastion of male supremacy. For one thing, the wives were very much part of the team, with gifts of their own to offer. From the beginning, the vision was about the *laos,* the laity and the building of community. There was already a small worshipping community at the Methodist church in Lancaster Road following a fairly traditional pattern of church meetings and activities. The three ministers respected and cared deeply for this faithful group of people who held together the everyday, essential routine work on buildings, finance, pastoral care and stewarding, thus freeing up the group ministry for exploration and outreach. Again, this was not simply one-way; the openness of the team meant that from the outset there was a mutual giving and receiving of pastoral support.

It was also one of the few churches which opened its doors to receive the newly-arrived West Indian immigrants and soon gained a reputation in the area as a 'welcoming church'.

The burning question, however, remained: what would be the shape of this new expression of church? The need was clear for all to see; how to set about it was far from straightforward. Slowly, a common mind began to emerge. There were several thousand West Indians and West Africans living in Notting Hill, of whom literally hundreds were Methodists. Although a small minority of these immigrants and their families had attended the Sunday services, especially in the mornings, there had been no great influx of new members. A systematic campaign of contact through visitation was initiated based on the records of baptisms and marriages over the previous two years. Efforts were made to contact those who had drifted away. A group of laypeople undertook to visit West Indian families who were in need. Practical measures such as finding warm clothing for those who arrived in the depths of an English winter, and helping with the search for jobs, accommodation, as well as assistance with claiming welfare benefits for those unaware of their entitlement to such aid. The re-decoration and equipping of two shabby vestries to form one large office, open every morning of the week, was an essential step forward. People knew that the church door was open, someone was always there and so they called in. This was in stark contrast to the rejection often experienced by immigrants, epitomized by a famous BBC radio programme in the middle 1960s, entitled, 'No Outsiders Here'. Requests for help varied from the resolving of marriage difficulties, rent issues with recalcitrant landlords, the address of a good solicitor, or the Citizens Advice Bureau, to enquiries about baptisms and weddings. Thus did these small beginnings lay down a pattern for the emerging work of the Group Ministry and provided a catalyst for the social revolution of the 1960s and 1970s in the streets and houses of Notting Hill. Of those early days, David Mason wrote, 'We had begun to find our true vocation and the work became as thrilling and satisfying as anything that could be undertaken.'[6]

[6] *News from Notting Hill: The formation of a group ministry*, p. 16.

What does Mr Ainger do?

By the time Geoff arrived in 1962 these early initiatives were under way. By his own admission he spent the first few months feeling semi-redundant as he struggled to find his role. With a wry smile he told the story of how, when Dr Colin Roberts, Head of the Home Mission Department visited Notting Hill, he was surprised to find just a handful of folk at the mid-week communion service. Later he asked the church member who was driving him back to the station, 'and what *does* Mr Ainger do?' – to which the reply was, 'he takes services and visits'! A fair description of the bread and butter work of most ministers! But it was a role which Geoff shaped with imagination and insight to serve the development of the Group Ministry.

One of his first impressions of Notting Hill was its *vitality*. Comparing this with the experience of East Harlem, he said,

> there was more of a social mix in Notting Hill, which could be seen on the Portobello Road on any Saturday. One had the sense of the close proximity of different ethnic groups and social classes. East Harlem was more of a sink . . . more broken. Notting Hill was broken too, but not in the same way. Black young people found it almost impossible to move out of East Harlem and the sense of hopelessness was acute. There seemed to be more potential for genuine change in North London.

Geoff's gift for getting alongside people of all kinds made him ideally suited to the kind of pastoral visiting that the situation in Notting Hill required. He walked around the area and the local estates in his cassock and became known affectionately as 'Father Angel'! As the Group Ministry developed, a system of lay visitors was deployed which eventually grew in number to over a hundred. They were appointed by the church as Assistant Class Leaders. It was a response to a growing congregation in which the community roll, rather than the membership list, became the major unit of pastoral care. This community orientation cannot be stressed too strongly. Open-ness, inclusiveness was the essence of the Group Ministry's teaching and practice. In the West Indian community, infant baptisms were an opportunity to draw the whole extended family together, not only to talk about the meaning of the Sacrament but to get to know them and their life stories.

All the time, the Group Ministry was seeking to be responsive to social need. Sometimes this meant utilizing church premises, and other responses were based in the neighbourhood. For instance, one problem demanding a rapid response was that of young mothers with two or three children under school age who, living in grossly overcrowded conditions, were finding little respite from the incessant demands of the children on their time and energies. Save the Children agreed to supply a trained leader on two afternoons a week, equip the place with toys and cover fuel costs. In return, the church guaranteed to keep the basement hall clean and warm. This Play Centre eventually provided facilities for mornings and afternoons from Monday to Friday, a service that was in great demand. Something that in these days is a fairly normal part of the programme of many local churches was innovative at that time. Alongside this, an Adventure Playground was set up on an old bomb site, in the running of which some younger members of the church were involved and a member of the Group Ministry served on the committee.

God, politics, tenants and drains

Commenting on the 'ancient English heresy' that religion and politics don't mix, David Mason observed,

... local politics can be so dull! A ward meeting can be as boring and quarrelsome as any church meeting and all political parties have their awkward squads. Even so, the task of building close relationships with local political leaders has gone on, with the Group Ministry enjoying much help and friendship from the three former LCC Councillors, the MP, parliamentary candidates ... and Borough Councillors.[7]

All three members of the Group Ministry served at various times on management committees of local schools, including the Remand Home, co-operated in the running of youth clubs, and became involved in the multifarious organizations that served the northern end of Kensington. They believed that if the church is genuinely to become part of a neighbourhood it needs to revise its priorities and recognize the immense worth of this involvement. It goes without saying that such engagement was time-consuming and made huge demands on the Group Ministry.

One of the most valuable activities with which the Group became associated was the Notting Hill Social Council, which co-ordinated much valuable work being done by churches and various social agencies in the area. This began in 1960 with David Mason as its first chairman, holding monthly meetings, and concentrating its attention on a study of the more outstanding social problems. One of its most enduring enterprises was the Portobello project, which began as a coffee bar for 'unattached' young people and developed a programme of outreach with its own premises and a trained youth leader. High on the Social Council's list of priorities was housing, which was described earlier in the chapter. In a very real sense this paved the way for the initiative of Bruce Kenrick, whose arrival

---

[7] *News from Notting Hill: The formation of a group ministry*, pp. 17–18.

in Notting Hill opened a new chapter in the Church's engagement with the chronic housing needs of the neighbourhood, vividly and movingly described by Labour politician, Alan Johnson, who grew up in Notting Hill in the 1950s.[8] Kenrick became an associate member of the Group and, believing that 'tenants, drains and other things' were the prime concern of God, founded the Notting Hill Housing Trust in 1963, putting his own home at risk by pledging it as security for the Trust's first purchase. This became a recurring pattern. Ken Bartlett, an Anglican priest who was to become Director of another nearby Housing Association, later wrote:

> The Trust took root when John Coward took *the amazing risk* (italics mine) of leaving his secure job with Richmond Council to direct the tiny precarious Trust. They were followed by others: the story of the Trust could be told in terms of the people who took personal risks in pursuit of a vision. Visions are useless if not shared.

Tackling homelessness: the launch of Shelter

In 1966, Bruce Kenrick launched Shelter as the national campaign for homeless people. Around the same time and by some extraordinary co-incidence, the ground-breaking TV documentary 'Cathy Come Home', written by Jeremy Sandford and directed by Ken Loach, was shown to British audiences around the country. Its dramatic portrayal of the plight of young homeless families, and the brutal treatment meted out by landlords and public officials, shocked decent people in all walks of life. Consequently, when Shelter was launched ten days later in central London it received huge publicity. Over the seven years from 1967, Shelter made grants totalling £262,000 to

---

[8] Alan Johnson, *This Boy*, Bantam Press, 2013.

the Notting Hill Housing Trust, which over its 50-year history has provided 27,000 affordable homes. This is a magnificent achievement but at least as significant has been its role in creating and maintaining socially mixed communities. The full story of the Notting Hill Trust is told vividly in Chris Holmes' book, *The Other Notting Hill*, in which he pays fulsome tribute to Bruce Kenrick both in the founding of the Trust and the emergence of Shelter. Without him they would never have happened. Bearing in mind Kenrick's crucial influence in the formation of the Group Ministry, first through the East Harlem Protestant Parish and later through his pioneer work in Notting Hill, it is important I think to pay this tribute to a key figure in the larger story.

If all this seems a digression, it is an important one. The Notting Hill Group Ministry was a pioneer project, breaking new ground in a time of huge social upheaval and it is impossible to measure its significance without understanding the socio-economic context in which it grew and developed.

Transforming the congregation: celebrating community

At the heart of this project was a worshipping multi-ethnic community and it is to this that we now turn. In March 2004, Geoff gave an interview for an Oral History Project conducted by the North Kensington Community Archive about the Notting Hill Group Ministry. The interviewer asked him about the worship at Lancaster Road during the 1960s. Geoff paused and then said, 'I remember the *hilaritas*, the joy. A lot of laughter. In the midst of all the tension and stress, there was an undercurrent of *celebration*.'[9] The church is primarily a grateful, celebrating community; at its heart is the incredible story of the God who loves the world utterly, a love manifested in the life, death and

[9] *Oral History Project*, Lancaster Road Methodist Church, 2004.

resurrection of Jesus, whose spirit is with us. Geoff often spoke about the sheer unpredictability of Sunday morning worship. For one thing, you simply didn't know who was going to turn up! He loved to tell the story of the Orthodox Bishop who having travelled in Africa was returning to his diocese in New York. The Notting Hill taxi driver, noting his dress, assumed that he wanted the local Orthodox church, but when the Bishop said that he was on holiday and was looking for a church of another persuasion, the cabbie deposited him outside the red doors of the Methodist church! Although Bishops were not spotted on a regular basis, there were visitors on most Sundays who were always made welcome, asked to bring greetings and invited to communal lunch following the service. And new people from the local community were also finding their way in. Someone who was part of the church at this time recalls:

> the excitement of those days as the congregation grew, mainly West Indians, but also people from Africa and other parts of the world. A tradition developed at the Harvest Festival when members of the congregation would stand up representing their countries of origin beginning with a different letter of the alphabet … a truly international community. Donald Eadie always chose Y for Yorkshire!

As noted above, the keynote was inclusiveness and as always Geoff was keen to point up its theological undergirding: 'The church must be serious at the centre – serious about its liturgy and sacraments, but porous at the edges … enabling freedom to move in and out.'

The Group Ministry evolved a pattern of Sunday morning worship, which included a regular celebration of the Eucharist, a monthly baptismal service and, on one Sunday in the month, a freer form of worship. They took seriously the meaning of the word 'liturgy' – from the Greek, *leitourgia*, meaning 'the service of the people'. It was worship rooted in the gospel and fully engaged with Notting Hill and the wider world. One frequent expression of this was, to use the 'prayers of concern', to focus on particular community needs. So, for instance, on a given Sunday, a social worker, or a teacher, would be invited to share something of their work, which was offered to God in the prayers – with a promise to pray regularly during the coming week for those particular situations. This emphasized the truth that there is no division between the sanctuary and the street, between worship and work, between sacred and secular. It is glory to God, in the High Street!

As time went on, the Group devised its own imaginative liturgies especially around the great Christian festivals of Advent, Christmas, Lent, Easter and Pentecost. A striking example of this was a Christmas celebration entitled, 'Ballad of the Homeless Christ'. It took the place of the sermon that evening. In preparation for the liturgy, the Group Ministry had gathered over 13 hours of recorded interviews on tape with families in the neighbourhood who had experienced the effects of homelessness and exploitation. These interviews, edited and reduced to 15 minutes of testimony, punctuated by statistics of London's homelessness, with songs sung to guitar, drum and clarinet accompaniment, combined to produce a powerful modern representation of the familiar Christmas story of the Christ who became a homeless refugee in Egypt.

A cry in the night and a child is born . . .
God makes our homelessness his home . . .

A similar format was used for a harvest festival, when exploring the theme of hunger and affluence in the world.

Songs from Notting Hill

The composing of new material was a vital aspect of this fresh approach to worship. Geoff led the music workshop, which, among other things, produced a collection entitled 'Songs from Notting Hill', some of which are in the Appendix. Stainer and Bell eventually published a number of these songs, making them available to a wider public. Though unable to read music, Geoff would hum the tune of the words of a song he had written to a pianist who then transcribed it as a musical composition! Members of this workshop included a number of young people who were studying in London colleges and universities and who became involved with the work of the Group Ministry at Notting Hill. Moira Duckworth was one of those students and recalls Geoff's influence on her developing Christian faith:

> I first met Geoff when I was twenty. I was in my first year at Southlands College in Wimbledon, training to be a teacher. Having tried the local Methodist Church ... I turned elsewhere for something to challenge me. I went to a meeting at Meth Soc (the students' Methodist Society) in Hinde Street and Geoff happened to be speaking. He was asking students to consider going to Notting Hill to help with the work there. He was appealing for help with youth work, one of his particular roles. A small group of us who were on a similar spiritual search began a journey which was to transform our lives. The work we did with Geoff alongside young people from the local estates mushroomed. His gift of communication with people of all ages and backgrounds was just remarkable. His ability to say profound, radical, challenging things in a simple way when preaching was exciting ... his last-minute preparation of Sunday morning's sermons was the source of a number of jokes, but eagerly anticipated! The way he

walked up and down at the front of the church waving that day's *Observer*, reading the headlines, referring to the lectionary readings then moving through thoughts connecting both, sometimes left me wanting a much longer sermon. Geoff's way with poetry and lyrics was a profound expression of his creative gifts and a means of communicating simply something of the essence of the gospel. I remember the Christmasses when 'Born in the night' and 'A cry in the night' were indeed born and how our family Christmas every year included those songs. Now the grandchildren are starting to sing them! All this led to the Music Workshop of which I was a singing member . . .

Geoff and the Music Group were invited to contribute to BBC Radio's 'Thought for the Day', and one member of the group spoke of the sense of excitement at being in a BBC session when they were recording one of Geoff's hymns.

Life in Community

Moira was one of a number of young Christians, mainly students, who became involved with Community House, a five-storey property in Blenheim Crescent (where the three ministers and their families had originally lived),

The house could accommodate up to 11 members in addition to the youth worker and his staff, with communal lounge and dining facilities. Members contributed a proportion of their income and shared equally in cooking and household duties. They supported the social and pastoral work of the Group Ministry, and were grounded in a discipline of regular prayer and celebration of the Eucharist. Not all were Methodists; in line with the ethos of the Group ministry, the Community was ecumenical in outlook. There was a regular

Sunday lunch where members held open house for visitors, mainly from the area but also from abroad, some of whom were given accommodation for shorter or longer periods. Keith Hiscock remembers, '. . . a blind young man from Hungary who had made his way out in their spring uprising, then feared to go back as Russia re-asserted its grip.' Keith also recalls 'a group of lonely, often mentally challenged older folk who were fed, visited, looked after when sick, and taken out in one of our succession of clapped out mini-buses. Many of them were great characters and vividly remembered.' Community House members set up 'the Blenheim Project', located on the central floor of the House and which existed to help drug addicts who had come into the area or those at risk arriving at London stations. Some were put up for short periods as support and listening time were offered. Geoff and the Group ministers were very supportive of this work.

When the House opened in August 1965, there was little or no furniture. Geoff gave them a piece of paper with a telephone number on it, indicating that the person might be able to help. The address was in Loughton. John Lampard recalls,

> We drove out one evening in the minibus we used. At the address we found a veritable treasure trove of second-hand furniture. We filled the vehicle with smaller items and tied wardrobes on the roof, probably in a highly dangerous way and returned with our booty to Notting Hill. It turned out that the owner, who had died, was a member of Geoff's former church in Loughton and the family were delighted to get the house cleared in a good cause. Geoff seemed a miracle worker.

Miracles both large and small seemed to happen on a regular basis.

Keith Hiscock, now a Methodist local preacher in Bedfordshire, was one of the students whose response to Geoff's call to help with the youth work at Lancaster Road changed the course of his life. He had intended to teach or follow research in historical geography, but through involvement with children and young people at Notting Hill decided that his vocation was in Child Care Social Work. He is one of a number of those who belonged to Community House whose life choices were profoundly influenced by those experiences. Some continued to live in the area; others have been involved in overseas projects. Keith writes,

> The legacy of Community House continues for many of us and Geoff's intellectual approach combined with deep feeling for humanity remains part of what we have carried with us. That Christ meets us in the encounters of the world is more than an idea. It is a real experience.

House Churches

In *News from Notting Hill*, the Group had written,

> Instead of regular meetings of 'classes' we are gradually establishing a network of house groups . . . we believe it is essential for the spreading out, the meeting outside which is involved in the house church idea.

The form of these house churches varied greatly; some would be devotional, with Bible study, singing and free prayer. This was true, though not exclusively, of those that met in West Indian homes; while in West African households, though singing was popular, there was more emphasis on discussing current affairs. Some groups watched TV programmes and discussed them. The common denominator of all these house churches was to focus on the life of their street or neighbourhood and to relate spiritual exercises to that reality. There was flexibility. Some emerged spontaneously out of a particular situation; others were more organised. Although the shape and purpose of these groups changed over the years, they continued to be an integral part of the Group Ministry's work.

Churches Together

Mention of community underlines the fact that although the Notting Hill Group Ministry was a Methodist project its vision was, from the outset, ecumenical. This was given concrete expression in the setting up of an ecumenical centre in the premises of Denbigh Road, the other Methodist Church in the neighbourhood. In 1967, David Mason described the Centre as 'something of a theological "wind-tunnel" through which people pass and where their assumptions and ideas are tested in discussion and exposure to the convictions of others'. It was about learning how to be Christians together in a big city; about living on a large map, a reminder that the word 'ecumenical' is not a 'churchy' concept. It comes from the old Greek word *oikumene*, meaning 'that which concerns the whole world'. Its 1970 annual report shows the Centre running courses and seminars on a wide range of issues, including Peace and Justice, Ageing, Communicating the Gospel in a pop-culture, Christ in the City, and 'Secular Pilgrimage' – a week's course for people on WCC scholarships from numerous denominational and national backgrounds, enabling them to learn by visiting social projects. An imaginative programme called 'City of God: City of man', enabled theological students from Catholic, Protestant and Orthodox traditions to spend a month together in July engaging in a hands-on, in-depth way with the life of the neighbourhood and learning from the dynamic interaction with one another and with the problems and potential of the city. A large number of groups and organisations both church and secular were using the premises on an occasional or regular basis, and the Centre fostered a growing range of ecumenical relations, local, national and international. Ivan Weekes, reflecting on the effective witness of Notting Hill churches and the Ecumenical Centre said, '. . . the local congregations rallied valiantly to support the Group Ministry through this long period in its stand for reconciliation in the face of community fear, race riots and in dealing with the local Notting Hill police.'

Fifty years on: Carnival and change

Recently, on a sunny January morning as I walked the streets of Notting Hill with Barbara, it was hard to believe that this neighbourhood had been so recently the centre of a major social revolution which had repercussions not only in London but nationwide. Chris Holmes described Notting Hill in the 1960s and early 1970s as 'tumultuous', marked by an extraordinary outburst, a 'cauldron' of community activity. It included tenants' organisations, the New Left Group, the Social Council, the Housing Trust and the Notting Hill Carnival. The Group Ministry was at the heart of this ferment.

The Carnival was – and is – a great community celebration. It began in a small way in 1965 and has developed into the largest street carnival in Europe, a unique, multi-racial event, with special importance for the Afro-Caribbean community across the capital and beyond. It grew annually in size and has assumed huge symbolic importance, especially for young black people who often experienced life on the streets as threatening and unsafe. For a once-marginalized community, it symbolized the fact that for a few days in the year, they *owned* Notting Hill. In spite of tensions and incidents over the years, often due to heavy-handed policing, the vast crowds were generally peaceful and exuberant. It was described by someone as 'a little bit of heaven on the streets'. When violence erupted at the Carnival during the late 1970s, the Rev. Donald Eadie, then a minister in Notting Hill, expressed the determination of the organizers to continue and praised the part played by local Methodists in helping to cool the situation and pick up the pieces. Those who had come to Notting Hill in the 1950s and 1960s from the Caribbean were now exercising leadership not only in church but also in the community.

On that January day, Barbara, who had worked for a Housing Trust in the North Kensington area during the growth of the Group Ministry, was able to interpret some of the changes of recent years. A certain amount of 'gentrification' *has* obviously taken place and the housing needs of today are different than those of the 1960s – for instance, increasing the provision of affordable homes for key public sector workers squeezed by an overheated London property market – and as a consequence helping to maintain socially mixed, sustainable communities. Today, Notting Hill is a multi-ethnic neighbourhood which remains a place where most residents want to live. Chris Holmes again: 'In a divided world it is an example of how people from many different backgrounds can and should be able to live together.'

We called in at the Methodist Church in Lancaster Road. Still largely unaltered on the outside, a later 'makeover' has changed the Victorian, galleried structure inside into a 'split-level' arrangement with the church upstairs, and meeting rooms on the ground floor. The basement is still in use and a community activity was in progress during our visit. Photographs in the vestibule indicated the still largely Afro-Caribbean make-up of the present congregation. At the front of the church is a tree planted in memory of Bruce Kenrick and, around it, workmen were creating a garden, which seemed to symbolize not only continuity with the past but a sign of hope in the present and for whatever future may lie ahead.

As we left, I was reminded of some words of Geoff, which appear at the end of a book he wrote during those early days in Notting Hill:

> The call to respond to what God is doing in the world today is a call into insecurity. It is a call into a spontaneity of ministry which can only be adequately described in terms of the work of the Holy Spirit and of a servant community which has begun to live the life of faith. Bonhoeffer said it was about watching with Christ in Gethsemane ... participating in his sufferings in the world. That is also the path to freedom for the Church in this or in any other day.[10]

---

[10] Geoffrey Ainger, *Jesus Our Contemporary*, SCM Press, 1967.

FOUR

Jesus Our Contemporary

We must persevere in quiet meditation on the life, sayings, deeds, suffering and death of Jesus in order to learn what God promises and what he fulfils.

(Dietrich Bonhoeffer)

During those momentous years, especially in East Harlem and Notting Hill, Geoff's understanding of Jesus was growing and changing. The 1960s was a time of serious questioning about the Christian Faith – not just by outsiders but by those inside the church. In *Honest to God,*[11] a book published in 1963, Bishop John Robinson shared his personal doubts – and his conviction that 'our image of God must go'. It sent shock waves through the church. Other theologians spoke of 'the death of God', invoking Bonhoeffer's striking phrase 'religionless Christianity'. In Rome, Vatican Two was shaking up the Catholic Church and on the African continent, nations were shaking off the yoke of colonialism. This was the 'swinging sixties'. . . . a time pregnant with new possibilities and dangerous opportunities.

Who is Christ for us today?

In 1965 Geoff led a retreat for SCM workers in which he explored the question: 'Who is Christ for us today?' – another of Bonhoeffer's memorable sayings. As a result of this he was asked to write a book based on the lectures given at the retreat.

---

[11] John Robinson, *Honest to God*, SCM Press, 1963 (new edition, 2009).

It was entitled *Jesus Our Contemporary*[12] and, although written 50 years ago, it still comes across with freshness and relevance. The chapter headings are striking: 'Jesus the Victim', 'The Man for Others', 'Jesus the Secular Believer', 'The Man for Me', 'The Man from Nazareth', 'The Head of His Body the Church'. The book, just 128 pages long, is a striking example of Geoff's ability to paint vivid word-pictures and use telling illustrations to illuminate the points he was trying to get across.

Writing of this volatile period, Geoff said,

> ... I was deeply indebted to the work of great New Testament scholars and theologians who shook me out of my youthful, inadequate certainties, through puzzlement, into real excitement in the presence of him who could sit enthroned in splendour above the altar in Coventry Cathedral, yet pass un-noticed in the crowded street, the 'Man for Others'. In the context of 'Honest to God' and 'Secular Christianity', I felt I not only had to respond to the challenge of such movements but also to write of Jesus as the 'Justified Celebrant' whose fundamental joy was rooted in the reality of God the Father. *The Jesus I came to know seemed to insist that the church was first of all a party, a feast, a celebration before it ever became a crusade.*

The chapter entitled 'The Justified Celebrant' fills out the picture.

> I find every attempt to 'spiritualize' the Beatitudes unconvincing. I find here, not a description of an idealized Christian, but a reference to the ordinary people who lived, worked, hoped and were exploited in 1st-century Galilee ... they carry that quality of *hilaritas,* of joyful

---

[12] Geoffrey Ainger, *Jesus Our Contemporary*, Seabury press, 1967.

certainty in the midst of insecurity which seems to fly in the teeth of the plain evidence of human experience. Yet Jesus dared to celebrate the plight of his fellow-human beings and challenge them to a way of living which can only be described either as plain foolish or as an expression of a fundamental celebration of their real situation. We all have problems with this man who was apparently sufficiently serious about his convictions to die for them, and yet who repeatedly gives the impression that he finds it hard to keep a straight face when confronted by our pieties . . . we always have a terrible time when we try to turn Jesus into a tragic hero. Osborne's Jimmy Porter wants a warm thrilling voice to cry out, 'Alleluia! I'm alive!' The teaching of Jesus about the Kingdom, about spontaneity and love and about angels' joy which undermined the weary solemnities of his day, surely echoed some such meaning; Alleluia! I'm alive! Alleluia, You're forgiven! Alleluia! You're cared for! The very hairs of your head are numbered.

Geoff was of the opinion that God's favourite word is 'yes'!

Eccentric community

The final chapter of *Jesus Our Contemporary* is about the church and its public ministry.

In another place, Geoff had said:

The church, to be true to its calling, must become 'the eccentric community', not because it is odd or different from others, but because he who is at the centre of its life stands outside its doors among the lost, 'the friend of publicans and sinners', as he was in Palestine long ago. In this respect, baptism became very important to me as the *sacrament of eccentricity*, of fundamental identification with the Christ who refuses to leave his sinful, ambiguous 'lost' world to seek safety among the saved. In the 1940s there was a terrible irony in the fact that Simone Weil, the young French philosopher, who had become a Christian, refused baptism precisely for this reason – that it would become a hallmark of respectability and separate her from the mass of 'godless' people in the industrial suburbs of Paris.

Geoff began that final chapter with a startling illustration. In July 1966, the members of the World Council of Churches' Conference on Church and Society had met in St Peter's Cathedral in Geneva to discuss the implications of the coming of Jesus for the world today.

But the pulpit on that Sunday morning was empty. The preacher was to have been Dr Martin Luther King, but he had cancelled his trip to Geneva to mediate in the race riots which had swept through Chicago the previous week. The sermon had been tele-recorded so that the Conference members could see and hear the preacher who was absent. Geoff remarked,

> It must have been a long time since the splendid pulpit of St Peter's spoke with such eloquence. Religionless Christianity does not mean dis-embodied Christianity. But there are no easy alternatives. Those of us who still believe in the Church, and who think of it as the Body of Christ, must look long and hard at that empty pulpit. The Church depends for its very life on *being where Christ is.*

Copernican revolution

Behind all this fresh and stimulating thinking was a discovery Geoff had made during a summer holiday, which amounted to something of a Copernican revolution in his understanding of the gospel. And it was Karl Barth who opened the door.

My understanding of Jesus led me then to turn faith upside down. All my perception of faith had been in terms of my having faith in God. True, I had been taught that faith was God's gift, but somehow the possibility of my having faith in Christ had remained a central theological proposition. *Now I came to find in Jesus the fundamental statement of God's faith in me and in all humanity.* Golgotha became supremely the place at which our faithlessness is only outmatched by the amazing faithfulness of God. I remember the shattering experience of reading, one summer holiday, Barth's chapters on Election, in which he turned Calvin upside down and helped me, for one, to a new understanding of faith.

Justified by our reliance on God's faith in us! Ultimately, the only rock which around the shifting sands of time and circumstance provides any kind of solid ground.

Before long, however, even that solidity appeared to be in real danger of losing its rock-like permanence.

FIVE

Exile

Exile is . . . the crippling sorrow of estrangement . . . the perilous territory of not belonging . . . a discontinuous state of being.

(Edward Said[13])

In the late 1960s, Geoff Ainger was at the zenith of his considerable powers as a preacher, worship leader, theologian and teacher. His communication skills had been recognized far beyond Notting Hill; he was a regular broadcaster on both BBC Radio and London Weekend Television; his involvement in the Ecumenical movement through the World Council of Churches led to an invitation to be part of the Methodist team on the first unity conversations with the Church of England. He seemed destined to become one of the outstanding Christian leaders of his generation.

World traveller

His ability to communicate with children and teenagers led to his appointment as chaplain to a World Methodist Youth Conference at Kingswood school which brought together 400 young people from all over the world. In 1969 he was a delegate to the WCC Youth Assembly in Australia, which gave him the opportunity to travel to other parts of the globe both before and after the meetings. He visited the Indian city of Calcutta and a number of other Asian countries, including Singapore and

---

[13] Edward W. Said, *Reflections on Exile*, Granta, 2001, p. 177.

Malaya. He ended the trip in the United States, visiting Chicago and Los Angeles, and took the opportunity to renew his acquaintance with East Harlem. In his own inimitable way, Geoff described the experience as 'split-level orbit'. The article he wrote on his return is full of incisive social comment. Australia was:

> . . . a great country whose history lies in the future, whose present is suspended between British roots, American protection, Asian threat and promise . . . whose fundamental shortages are of fresh water and people . . . churches which did not seem to have become part of the 'national way of life' in the way the American churches have.

Of America he wrote:

> . . . a society of brilliant intelligence and massive prejudice, extraordinary achievement and persistent failure, impressive religion amidst an all-pervading atmosphere of violence.

Though it had been a remarkable time, he admitted that he was glad to be back home. But home too was part of this split-level world.

Eye of the storm

As the decade drew to a close, storm clouds were gathering. They would eventually break, with devastating consequences for Geoff, his family and the Notting Hill congregation.

Over a period of time he had become deeply unhappy in his marriage, to such an extent that he felt unable to remain in the marital home, although initially he continued to be part of the Group Ministry and was in regular contact with his children, Margaret, David and Paul (born in Notting Hill). The tensions were tearing him apart, leading to eventual breakdown and to his subsequent resignation from ordained ministry in 1973.

In a paper he wrote some years later for the *Epworth Review,* Geoff described the deep, dark valley through which he passed at this time. It seems fitting to quote his own words here.

> My breakdown, that 'passing through the waters', became not a splendid epic of faith, but a frightful, desperate and undignified ordeal of mud and storm and terror, of guilt and loneliness in which the familiarities of Jesus and community fell away, and were pushed away, leaving me to scramble on to the shore of the wilderness, a survivor. It was not so much an entry into the wilderness *as being invaded by the wilderness,* an experience of having no perimeter defences against the incursion of despair, guilt and horror.

This is strong language and the gravity it describes is underlined by the next sentence,

> Yet even in that experience I was aware of those waves of flint and grit breaking on some inner bastion, some core of my person which was not overwhelmed. Presumably that is what separated me from those who commit suicide. To be invaded by the wilderness totally must spell the death of the self.

Geoff needed to know what was happening to him and why. His initial response was brutally honest. 'In my scramble through the waters I lost my simplicity. In my guilty innocence I felt I could only defend the truth by telling lies, only hang on to faithfulness by breaking promises, only defend the fundamental integrity of a new experience of loving by having to face the reality of my having failed to sustain a loving relationship.'

He was going into exile . . . a long way from home. In

physical terms exile is an experience that affects millions of people on the planet. Ours is the age of the refugee. Displaced people with little or no prospect of ever returning home, armed only with a ration card and an agency number. No-one in our own time has written about this condition more perceptively than Edward Said the Palestinian scholar and activist, who lived most of his adult life as an exile in America. He wrote, 'Exile is a terrible experience. It is the unhealable rift forced between a human being and a native place . . . between the self and its true home. It is the perilous territory of not belonging, of being cut off from one's roots . . . nothing is secure.' He went on to say, 'the word refugee has become a political one, whereas "exile" carries with it a touch of solitude and spirituality.'[14]

Innocence and guilt

Over the following months, Geoff spent many hours in therapy. During this process, the psychiatrist explored with him the possible meanings of an incident that happened when he was just over two years old. He contracted diphtheria and was taken to an isolation hospital. His parents were not allowed to see him for the first ten days, and only once a week for the following six weeks. During the first period of his stay in that hospital he refused to speak, until towards the end of it, he apparently stood up in his cot and began to sing his childish version of 'Onward Christian soldiers'. After that he communicated normally with nurses on the ward. But when his parents came, he greeted his father but refused to recognize his mother. And in that cinema where the teenage Geoff became conscious of a call to ministry, Stanley wakes up on his first morning at Ujiji and finds Livingstone rehearsing a choir of boys in the hymn, 'Onward Christian Soldiers'!

[14] *Reflections on Exile*, p. 177.

Was there some deep mysterious connection between Geoff's breakdown and possible meaning of that hospital experience – meanings which would have to be expressed in terms of 'abandonment', 'murderous hatred', 'guilt'; a silent, frightening wilderness from which the child signified his emergence with a song? Interestingly his father had died around the time of his breakdown.

Geoff commented, 'whether the psychiatrist's interpretation of this myth from my early childhood was correct I am not in a position to say. But I was left with a new questioning.

When theologians sing,

Out of the depths I cry to thee
Lord God, O hear my prayer

could they be putting into words the unspoken cry of a child trapped between innocence and guilt, without words and yet somehow being heard?'

When he articulated those thoughts in 1977, Geoff was only just beginning to emerge from that dark place. To all intents and purposes he had lived for several years outside the life of the church and had made the surprising discovery that he did not need to go to church to survive, although he did 'drop in' at various services from time to time. Having arrived looking for bread, he confessed that 'with some splendid exceptions' he had been offered a stone. A stone 'which is highly polished and symmetrical remains inedible'. He relates what happened when he went to worship in a village chapel one Sunday morning. The young local preacher read from Acts 17 the story of Paul on Mars Hill and went on in his sermon to talk about the importance of relaxing on holiday! But as Geoff reflected on that story it seemed to suggest a 'not-knowing', an agnosticism that made possible, talk of resurrection. In his sense of remoteness from any form of 'blessed assurance' he put down his thoughts in a poem.

What was there in that shrine
To call forth talk of resurrection
Is there a 'not-knowing'
That gives birth to new beginnings?
What alchemy of doubt and piety
Leads us beyond our dying certainties
Toward surprise?
Dare we tend an altar lovingly
And yet confess we do not know?
'To the unknown God . . . '
To lover, child or neighbour . . .
A whole society I thought I knew.
Do I stand acolyte before an altar
Even to that part of me which lies
Beyond what I have known?
Could I pass from certainty
Towards the mystery we call
Resurrection?

'At the moment,' he wrote, 'the question mark is a sign of hope; for those who find it difficult to arrive at anything as robust as faith, there is a form of doubt which far from settling for cynicism or despair, at least keeps alive the awareness of the *possibility* of faith.'

Although separated from the church during this time, Geoff was not isolated from a number of good and generous friends, some of them from Notting Hill. Most of all, there was the 'new experience of loving', a reference to Barbara who was alongside him throughout the darkness of his depression, a strongly supportive presence, and who was to become his second wife. Her contribution to his eventual healing was considerable.

Wounded healer

Geoff was, in the words of Henri Nouwen, 'a wounded healer'. Later, he came to understand this stage of his journey in terms of the story of Jacob, whom he once described as that 'venal swine who cheated his brother out of his rightful inheritance'. There comes the moment of crisis when, years after that event, Jacob has to face his brother and the truth of what he has done. The story is told in the book of Genesis. As he contemplates the fateful encounter and the possibility of Esau's revenge the following day, he is left alone in the darkness to face his terror. In this state he is encountered by a mysterious stranger, who wrestles with him through the night. The stranger refuses to reveal his name, but assures Jacob that he will not be overcome and as a sign gives him a new name – Israel – one who prevails in the struggle. Here in his inner wrestling with the furies and the demons God meets him. But he is marked by the struggle and as the sun rises he limps towards his brother and a new future. Like Jacob, Geoff emerged from his searing wilderness experience to a new beginning, but marked, wounded.

In descriptions of his breakdown, the word 'guilt' keeps on recurring. One has the sense that, although he came through the ordeal, he never completely shook off the sense of guilt for the perceived consequences of his actions in the lives and relationships of those he loved the most. This is honestly and poignantly expressed in a poem, written later, linking Jacob's wrestling with his own:

SUNRISE OVER PENIEL

Why can't I get free
from some fundamental guilt
that runs its subterranean way
beneath the daylight of my days
and suppurates in dogged bouts
of clear hatred of myself?

I say 'fundamental'
yet, it is my faith that what is fundamental
is not my guilt
but the love of God who makes me in his image
and calls me by name.
Credo, I believe that Yes and No
are not in simple equipoise
Yes! and Yes again! Says the gospel of the crucified.
Why then, can I not leave behind
The undermining No?

Is it because when I am asked my name
The Jacob I have always been
cannot quite manage to be Israel overnight
and stride out strongly in the morning sun?
Lord, is my limping sure sign
that Jacob has not been simply left behind?
That princely Israel, sunlit on the path towards home
bears within himself the felt wounds of his journey
and of his becoming?

SIX

Return

Can God spread a table in the wilderness?

(Psalm 78:19)

*Christ has sanctified the desert and the wilderness shines
with promise.*

(Thomas Merton)

Geoff's re-habilitation took time. It was eight years before he
was re-instated as a Methodist minister and 11 years before
he took up another circuit appointment. By 1980, the Notting
Hill Group Ministry had been in existence for 20 years. That
period witnessed several changes in the ministerial staff; of those
who came with their families, no less than five experienced
marital breakdown and separation – a very high casualty rate
indeed. Although not all these failures can be attributed to
Notting Hill, the peculiar demands of this high-powered pioneer
ministry were undoubtedly a major contributory factor. All
ministers with pastoral responsibility for congregations know the
pressures of a vocation where it is tempting to allow the work of
the church to be a substitute for the claims of family and where
church members can sometimes unwittingly or deliberately
collude in this neglect. In Notting Hill, those pressures were
multiplied. It wasn't simply members of the congregation who
were under stress; it was the community with which the Group
Ministry was involved who were suffering the effects of poverty,
racism, mental health issues and family breakdown.

Candles of Failure

One of the most powerful liturgies used at Notting Hill, entitled 'Candles of Failure' became an essential part of the annual Lenten preparation for Easter. On each Sunday in Lent, a candle was lit to represent a particular failure of love, loyalty and forgiveness represented in the gospel accounts of the disciples' relationship with Christ and with each other . . . leading to what appeared to be the ultimate failure – the arrest, torture and judicial murder of Jesus himself. The question arises; in the light of the Biblical witness and the Christian story, what do we understand by 'failure'? I recall the acute sense of having let God and the people down in a church of which I was minister, through failure to resolve a particular situation and for which I took the blame. When I was struggling with this, a wise, retired minister spoke to me about 'the sacrament of failure'. On Easter Day, the candles are re-lit one by one – not to cancel out the darkness of betrayal, cowardice and denial – but to affirm that within failure faced with Christ lies the seed of new beginnings.

In the Bible, the wilderness is not only associated with loss and terror. It is also the place of encounter with the living God and the hope of renewal. God *does* spread a table even in the wilderness. There *is* a road out of the abyss.

In the meantime, Geoff needed to find work. He and Barbara had moved to Harlesden, where their son, Colin, was born. Later they went to live in Hemel Hempstead. Barbara was working for a Housing Trust and Geoff got a part-time job at Southwark college teaching further education students in English, Liberal studies and Religion. He worked for a Certificate in Education during his first year and continued teaching until his return to full-time ministry in 1984. He continued throughout to be in regular contact with his three older children. Geoff was a born teacher and enjoyed the challenge of engaging young minds in the pursuit of knowledge.

But as his recovery continued, part of him longed for a return to circuit ministry to which the sense of call was still strong.

About time

A story which Geoff told many times, concerns his return to Notting Hill, after an absence of several years, out of the ministry and feeling under something of a cloud. As he climbed the church steps, not knowing how he would be received, he prepared for the worst. At the top was Ela Barnard, a lifelong member of the congregation, in her eighties by now, strait-laced and grim of aspect, being blind in one eye. With her good eye, she looked him up and down and said . . .

About time too!

SEVEN

Servant of the Word

Geoff Ainger is one of the ten best preachers in the world.
(Albert van den Heuvel)

When van den Heuvel wrote those words in the 1960s he was a secretary of the World Council of Churches and had heard a fair number of preachers. It is quite a tribute.

When we were planning this book, we entertained the idea of including a selection of Geoff's sermons in an appendix, but knowing how uninspiring even the best sermons can be in cold print, we abandoned the idea. It was Barbara who came up with the suggestion of making a selection from his recorded sermons and putting them on a CD that could be included inside the back cover of the book. There is no shortage of material as many of his sermons from the Orpington days were recorded on tape and friends from that time, Peter and Margaret Daone, kindly agreed to undertake the task of making the selection for inclusion on the CD. Peter is one of several who, over the years, were inspired by Geoff to offer for ordained ministry.

Preaching and imagination

Many of those who read this book will have memories of Geoff's preaching. It is a tribute to any preacher (and a surprise!) when someone says in conversation, 'I remember . . . that sermon you preached . . .'. It doesn't happen too often. I suppose I must have heard Geoff preach a dozen times over the years I knew him. I can recall most of those sermons; more importantly, some changed my way of seeing a particular text or passage of Scripture. Just one example: He was preaching one Sunday morning in Lichfield on the text in Matthew 4 which quotes Isaiah's prophecy, 'The people who walked in darkness have seen a great light . . .' He told the story of one Good Friday when he was invited to give a five-minute talk in a local cinema between film showings – which was not unusual in the 1950s, especially in cinemas owned by the Rank Organisation. The manager asked Geoff if he would like to be spotlighted in the darkened theatre. He politely declined, saying that he would like the house lights turned on so that he could see who was present in the audience! He went on to say that Jesus wanted the light to shine not on himself but the people . . . especially the outsiders, the rejected and the poor . . . the ones for whom he had come.

Geoff was in the great Methodist evangelical preaching tradition; rooted in the gospel, and in his own wide, deep experience of life. He was a striking example of that oft-quoted adage that preachers should read Bible and newspaper together, never in a shallow way but always to illuminate the truth he was trying to convey, helping his hearers to perceive God's activity in contemporary events, whether local, national or international. Passionate, eloquent and prophetic, stirring the imagination, challenging the mind and will. Refusing to settle for glib certainties, he insisted that the questions are often more important than the answers – especially those questions put to us by God. And always that sense of the generous abundant grace of God. He said to me more than once, 'never forget that in every congregation there is at least one person who is just desperate for a word which will help them get through the next week'. He knew because he had been there himself.

We decided to include one written sermon – partly because it was not recorded, but mainly because it was the last sermon Geoff preached. It was the occasion of the re-opening of the restored church at Lichfield in September 2012. He knew he had only weeks to live and he was unable to stand, but he readily accepted the invitation. He reminded us that the church lives by a story – the story of our humanity touched by transcendence. It is the role of the minister and by implication, the role of the congregation – to be responsible for the story.'

It is a powerful word and may serve as Geoff's last will and testament to the Church.

In an age when preaching has become devalued in some parts of the church, Geoff said, 'I only plead that preaching be taken seriously by preachers who will risk exploration, sharing and to a degree, confession, with those who listen.'

Orpington: return to circuit ministry

His last appointment before retirement was to the suburban town of Orpington in Kent, which gave the opportunity for a sustained preaching ministry over an eight-year period.

All the sermons included in the CD come from that time. In the 1980s, Orpington Methodist Church was a thriving and growing congregation. Geoff and Thelma Underwood who now live in Lichfield were members at the time. Thelma recalls,

> Orpington was a large church with a membership approaching 250. There were many activities, including a big Sunday school, uniformed organisations, a youth club, house groups and a dramatic society. It was an outward-looking community. An annual sponsored walk initiated by Aileen Cuckson in the 1960s had enabled scores of young people to do voluntary work abroad and in Britain, sometimes in groups. An ongoing link has been forged with the Matthew Rusike Hospital in Zimbabwe.
>
> Members of the church included professional people, teachers and others with organisational and leadership skills. Orpington was blessed with a succession of

extraordinarily dedicated and gifted ministers over the years who carried the work forward. We needed someone who could hold it all together and inspire. Geoff more than fulfilled the criteria; moreover, his preaching, Bible teaching and pastoral work brought a new vision of what Christian discipleship means in the 20th century and beyond.

Geoff and Barbara became fully involved in the varied life of the church and circuit. They were regular participants in the annual walk; one incident illustrates Geoff's sense of fun and his talent for spinning a good yarn, which lost nothing in the telling! On the year in question the route of the walk passed through a field at the top end of which a herd of cows were grazing. According to Geoff all the walkers had detoured the field in order to avoid the cows. 'But I,' he said, 'I carried a stick, and I approached the cows giving one of them a sharp tap. And behold, just as the sea opened before Moses, so the cows parted and I passed through the midst of them unharmed. Better still, when I reached the stile and looked back, behold, they had come together again!'

Leipzig; this wall will fall

There are a number of striking features about the Orpington sermons. One is the fact that if you knew nothing of the history of the period you could gain from them a good idea of contemporary world events, especially those happening in Europe, during that remarkable decade which saw the collapse of communism and the dismantling of the Berlin Wall. In the early months of 1989, Geoff visited Leipzig, then part of East Germany. He was on a Sabbatical and stayed with a German pastor and his wife, Frieder and Monika Hammermüller. In one of their many conversations, Geoff said to Frieder, 'this wall will come down', to which Frieder replied with conviction, 'Not in my lifetime.' Before the end of the year the wall did indeed fall, and a new chapter in German and European history began. It was also the beginning of a friendship between the Aingers and the Hammermüllers that developed over the next few years through a number of reciprocal visits. A link was also forged between Leipzig and Orpington, again with mutual exchanges. Of this friendship, Frieder commented in a letter to Geoff just before he died,

> . . . and that you came behind the Iron Curtain in June 1989, bringing hope we couldn't believe in, and saw us again together with Barbara and the Underwoods after the wall came down later that year and invited our family to Orpington . . . you made us rich and we are very, very grateful.

Frieder was present at Geoff's farewell service at Orpington in 1992, when he preached on the word 'Amen'. In the conclusion he exclaimed, 'The word Amen is not a folding of the arms and a nodding of the head. It is about kicking open a door into the future!'

Another notable feature of that period is the number of sermons he preached on baptism. Each time the sacrament was included in the morning service was an opportunity to point to its significance not only for the church but for the world. For Geoff it was a dramatic proclamation of the gospel; of God's affirmation of our humanity, our essential goodness, our destiny . . . of his fundamental faith in us . . . Christ reaching out to embrace us with unconditional love, long before our response. When preparing for his funeral he asked that these affirmations and responses be included in the liturgy. Like Luther, who when he was severely tested and tempted to deny that he was held in the love and mercy of God, would declare 'I have been baptized!'

Creative Bible study

When I came to Lichfield in 2004, I was looking for a meeting that would offer some serious Bible study. Little did I know what riches awaited me! Almost as soon as I arrived Geoff invited me to join a group that met in his home on alternate Thursday mornings.

We would begin with coffee at 10.30 am, followed by an hour of study, ending with lunch at 12 noon. Often there would be 20 or more people packed into the Aingers' living room; occasionally standing room only seemed to be called for, but everyone was eventually seated! Thursday mornings at Curborough Road were eagerly anticipated and we were rarely disappointed. To sit at Geoff's feet was to be stimulated, inspired, challenged and fed by a gifted teacher who not only knew the central themes of the Bible but had a profound understanding of the modern world and a rare perception of how one interacted with the other – all done with flair and imagination. It revealed the barren-ness of the fundamentalist, literalist approach to the Bible which simply does not take Scripture seriously enough. Later, Geoff asked me if I would share in the leading of the sessions – another example of his generosity.

It is difficult to convey the ethos of those meetings to those who weren't there. Geoff's easy informal style meant that no-one was intimidated and he would often begin with an anecdote or funny story; with Geoff, humour was never far away. But after the coffee, chat and a short prayer, we were left in no doubt that we were there to think and to engage with the Bible in a serious way. His method was to use themes, each series consisting of five or six sessions. We did a series in the autumn and another between January and March. The titles of some of these series give an idea of the flavour: 'Below-stairs theology'; 'Paul as an agony uncle'; 'To give us fresh eyes';[15] 'The shaping of our desires' (a series on the Lord's prayer); 'Miracles – a human possibility'; 'The power of the powerless'; and 'The Body Language of God'. For every session Geoff produced a paper that was distributed beforehand and we were invited to share in the reading of the passages. Part of his genius was to help us to see the relationship between Old and New Testaments in the context of the Bible's central message and its relevance for now. Once, he was re-telling the story of the disciples on the road to Emmaus. 'In the depth of their grief and sadness they had not forgotten to show hospitality to a stranger . . .', then he paused and took us back to the book of Genesis, to Abraham and Sarah, wondering where their next meal was coming from and how on earth the incredible promise of God that they had embraced could possibly come true . . . suddenly there are three strangers outside their tent, with whom they share the little food they have . . . 'the promise is renewed and in the face of impossible odds a new future opens for the people of God'.

> We saw a stranger yesterday
> We put food in the eating place, drink in the drinking place
> Music in the listening place
> And in the sacred name of the Triune God
> he blessed us . . . our house . . . and our dear ones.
> As the lark says in her song:
> often, often, often, goes the Christ in the stranger's guise.
>
> (Celtic Rune of Hospitality)

---

[15] This is included in Appendix One.

Not always fully appreciated, perhaps, was his depth of scholarship, the breadth of his reading and undergirding it all, a lifetime's experience of darkness and light, sorrow and joy, despair and hope, dead ends and new beginnings. If not always articulated, we left those Thursday mornings saying, 'our hearts have been warmed again as he opened the Scriptures to us!'

GOLD STANDARD (a poem for Geoff)

I gave you gold
for Christmas . . .
something symbolic in that?
Maybe. But in reality
it was 'fool's gold'
and neither of us
were fooled!

But today
another, truer symbolism
came to mind.

For me and I know
for others,
you are the
gold standard.
Many times we came to
your table
looking for bread.
You never short-changed us
offering stones
instead.

You were the alchemist
changing the base currency
of our dullness
into nuggets of pure gold
making us rich
beyond measure.

(WRB 31/12/12)

EIGHT

The Listener

I came to understand that the Church is primarily a hearing community . . .

Geoff and I shared a passion for the writing of RS Thomas the great Welsh poet who died in 2000. We did a session together in the Darwin Society some years ago on 'The Divine as artist and mathematician in the poetry of RS Thomas'. In it we explored some of the images of God suggested by this theme; the attentiveness that the creator brings to her task, almost in an attitude of waiting for the painting or piece of music to suggest the next notes or brush-strokes. Thomas spoke of keeping within 'listening distance of the silence we call God' and that 'the meaning is in the waiting'. In a society that attaches such importance to action and tangible results this is highly counter-cultural. Thomas Merton wrote, 'We live in a state of constant *semi-attention* to the sound of voices, music, traffic or the generalized noise of what goes on around us all the time. We are not fully present and not entirely absent.'[16] Although Geoff would not have described himself as a contemplative he knew the value of reflection and attentiveness.

Retreats

In retirement he was part of a team which ran courses for ministers and their spouses who were about to superannuate. He was also in demand as a leader of ministerial retreats. One

---

[16] Quoted in Kathleen Deignan (ed.), *A Book of Hours*: *Thomas Merton*, Sorin Books, 2007, p. 148.

for which I have the complete notes includes six sessions on the theme of 'Playful Remembering: Ministry in a post-modern age'. It is a masterclass in Geoff's gift for lateral thinking and his stress on the importance of imagination in our approach to the Bible, theology and ministry. He quotes Margaret Guenther, who says,

> our culture has made leisure an industry but knows very little about play. Often, what is called 'play' is compelled, competitive and compulsive. I am constantly struck by the proximity of 'play' and 'pray' ... Sometimes this is brought home to me when using my word processor. My fingers take on a life of their own and I find myself writing, 'it will be necessary to *play* about this'![17]

From Manningtree to Lichfield

Geoff retired in 1992 to Manningtree, Essex, his home county, although Barbara continued her work, commuting to London. Geoff had come full circle. The circuit included the village of Mistley where he was born. David and Nancy Shearmur, leaders of the church at Manningtree, have written of Geoff, '... he made a great contribution to our church and the local community, with his preaching, visiting and concern for everyone he met and knew.' They pay tribute to his legacy in the encouragement of creative Bible Study and the use of church buildings to serve the local community. When the church celebrated its 200th anniversary in 2007, Geoff was asked to write a hymn to mark the occasion. The hymn, 'There is no beginning to God's love', set to the tune 'Manningtree' is included in Appendix Two.

---

[17] Margaret Guenther, *Holy Listening: The art of spiritual direction*, Darton, Longman and Todd, 1993, p. 60.

They also refer to Geoff's sense of fun, recalling an incident when the local choral society, on a visit to the German-partnered town of Kessel, attended the thermal baths. Geoff, without hesitation queued for the sauna, but feeling somewhat under-dressed wondered if he ought to wear his dog collar! He was seen with different eyes after that! He had been a member of the Probus Club in Manningtree and before he left they gave him a send-off lunch. The group met in an upstairs room of the Red Lion pub. In his response Geoff said.

> When five years ago I came to Manningtree as a lifelong follower of the friend of publicans and sinners, I had asked the question, 'where in this town can I find a bunch of experienced sinners meeting on publicans' premises?' The answer was clear . . . the Probus Club, upstairs at the Red Lion!

It was just another example of his delightful sense of humour, but also pointed to another of Geoff's qualities – the ability to get alongside folk of all sorts. He was a *kind* man, genuinely interested in people. When he asked, 'how are you?' it was not a perfunctory question. You felt instinctively that you mattered to him.

Maureen and Dennis Scott ran a Christian Bookshop and café in Manningtree called the Mustard Seed, which was managed by members of Bradfield Methodist Church, together with committed volunteers, and quickly established itself as a regular meeting place; a welcoming environment, somewhere to eat, chat and share worries. They write,

> Geoff could be found there on most days, not only as a customer, but clearing tables, washing up, and scrubbing potatoes. Helpful as this was, he would always be on hand

to advise, recommend books, pray with, chat to, laugh with and always listen to anyone, of all faiths and none.

His ability to meet people in a way they felt comfortable with was invaluable ... raising their self-esteem. A customer said to us that if all Christians were like Geoff, then maybe there would be many more of them about!'

Manningtree however was not to be their final move. Geoff and Thelma Underwood had moved to Lichfield in 1997 to be near their daughter Alison and her family who had lived in the city for a number of years. Soon afterwards, the Aingers visited them and were impressed by Lichfield's cultural vitality and its position at the centre of their family network. They moved to Curborough Road in 1998 and were joined the following year by Barbara's mother Vera who settled happily into Lichfield life after her move from South Wales.

Lichfield is a Midlands city with a rich history. The Romans had a settlement there and the 7th-century saint, Chad, founded his church on the site of the present cathedral. Among Lichfield's famous sons are Samuel Johnson, one of the outstanding literary figures of the 18th century who compiled the first English dictionary; David Garrick, the dramatist who, like Johnson made his name in London; and Erasmus Darwin, the doctor and botanist, grandfather of the famous Charles. It was Erasmus Darwin's home which provided a meeting place for 'the Lunar Men', that group of brilliant inventors, entrepreneurs and industrialists whose work spawned the Industrial Revolution, transforming the face of Britain and the world. It is a good place to live and the Aingers were soon very much at home.

Attentive listening

Lichfield Methodist Church runs a coffee shop four days a week and, as at Manningtree, Geoff could often be found with his toast and coffee, 'loitering with intent'! Not that he was consciously engaging in 'outreach', but more often than not he was deep in conversation with a regular customer or someone who had just 'dropped in'. You could sense the quality of his listening and over the years more than a few people were helped. Someone described him as a gentle giant. His vulnerability was part of his strength and it was this which helped to make him such a fine pastor. Ivan Weekes, a member of the Notting Hill congregation, a West Indian who became vice-president of the Methodist Conference, said this of Geoff,

> His humour and genuine understanding of people and of the gutter in which many found themselves marked him out for me . . . on a personal note, Geoff was my mentor, my anchor and my friend. During my life, an experience almost like a storm threatened to blow apart the anchor of my faith and that of my family. Geoff not only ministered to us but held the light of restoration in a dark world.

It is a tribute to his pastoral gifts that when the Lichfield coffee shop was thinking of a name for a group of informal listeners they decided to call them 'aingers'!

Joys and sorrows

The years of retirement saw both sad and happy events. Around the time of Geoff's 80th birthday, his brother Peter, died of cancer only days after his wife Aileen who had cared for him during his illness. This was followed almost immediately by the death in hospital of his son David, who had struggled for some time with addiction problems. This death was particularly hard for Geoff and brought back to the surface those buried feelings of guilt which he had lived with down the years. It was a devastating time.

But there were joys too. Vera's 90th birthday was celebrated, as was daughter-in-law Caroline's ordination as a Methodist minister. Grandson Tim, Margaret and Duncan's son stayed with them often and within a space of three years there were four more grandchildren – Colin and Fran's sons, Felix and Hallam, and Paul and Caroline's two, Jarred and Ethan – all boys! Numerous holidays at home and abroad, were enjoyed with family and friends.

In 2009 Geoff was diagnosed with bowel cancer and underwent surgery. He recovered and for the best part of two years continued to lead an active life – though he had to give up golf, which was a pity as I had at last found a partner who was almost as bad as myself! I teased him about the fortunes of his beloved Norwich City and very occasionally he had bragging rights when they managed to beat Manchester United or hold them to a draw!

In 2011, a routine scan revealed more cancer activity, now in the liver and he began another course of treatment, which involved removal of the tumours by laser surgery followed by chemotherapy. In the late summer of 2012 his doctors told him that they would need to increase the dosage and that this might be accompanied by severe side-effects with no guarantee of long-term benefit. Approaching the age of 87, he decided that enough was enough. With Barbara's agreement, and after a family consultation, Geoff informed the hospital that he had decided to discontinue the treatment.

NINE

Last Days

Rembrandt was wrong!

In 2012 the family purchased a property in Yarmouth on the Isle of Wight. It was large enough for everyone to stay together and it meant that there would be memories of Geoff in a place that it was hoped would become a venue for family holidays over the years. Geoff did, in fact, enjoy several short stays during the spring and summer of 2012 and loved the place.

Still teaching

By the autumn it was obvious that he was approaching the final phase of his journey. When he could no longer stand, his bed was brought downstairs and the dining room became his bedroom. During this time, he was cared for magnificently by Barbara and together with GP daughter Margaret, who visited regularly, they organized a system of carers and nurses which meant that he was able to be at home until the end. They were ably supported by family, friends from church and the wider community, neighbours, and a constant stream of visitors.

At the beginning of Advent we arranged to celebrate the Eucharist. The Underwoods, with Alison and Barbara, gathered round his bed in the room where we had shared so many meals together, which seemed fitting as we recalled that meal which is 'a foretaste of the heavenly feast prepared for all humankind'. Geoff was deeply moved and the tears flowed freely. Later, as we chatted, he suddenly and without warning wagged his finger at us, as if preaching and exclaimed, 'Rembrandt was wrong!'

We were startled, wondering if this was some kind of brainstorm! But, he went on;

> when Rembrandt put on canvas his understanding of the parable of the prodigal son he got it wrong! And so has western Christianity. The son did not grovel at the feet of his static, scarcely stooping father! No! The story Jesus told reads, 'while the son was still far off, his father saw him and was filled with compassion; he ran, put his arms around him and kissed him'. And there was a feast to celebrate the home-coming.

For Geoff, this was not an academic point. It went to the very core of what Christian faith is all about.

So, we pause here to reflect more deeply on that story which we think we know but because of its very familiarity may have missed its central message. Kenneth Bailey[18] in his masterly exposition of the parable not only links it with the account of Jacob at Peniel, but suggests that it is in fact Jesus re-telling that story, the story of Israel. Jacob, of course, approached the encounter with his brother, Esau, not in any spirit of remorse or repentance but still plotting to save his life, the lives of his family and avoid the destruction of his property. So he sends gifts ahead, hoping to appease Esau and deflect his supposed anger. But as he approaches the meeting with trepidation his brother runs to embrace him. Similarly the prodigal, on his way back from the far country to the family home, having wished his father dead and made off with his share of the inheritance (which would in law have come to him only on his father's decease), is planning how he can cut his losses. He has squandered Dad's money and sunk to the ignominy of feeding

---

[18] Kenneth E. Bailey, *Jacob and the Prodigal: How Jesus retold Israel's story*, IVP Academic, 2003.

pigs. Now he has to find a way of surviving. He will grovel, but then will tell his father what he must do *for him*. 'Make of me a craftsman.' This is not repentance. As with Jacob it is about survival. Bailey asks us to see this through the lens of Palestinian culture in the time of Jesus and understand that the father's behaviour would have been seen as at best unlikely and at worst, disgraceful. The younger son had besmirched the family honour, insulted his father and was deserving of the most severe punishment. We see him in our mind's eye, exhausted and apprehensive, gritting his teeth at the prospect of the hostile reception that awaits him not only from his father, his brother, and the family servants, but the whole community. Arriving during daylight hours when he can be seen from a distance, he prepares to run the gauntlet down the narrow village street. To his surprise and shock he sees his father running the gauntlet *for him* in full view of the village. The *compassion*. which is usually taken to mean that the father felt sorry for the destitute state of his son, may be correct but the father also knows full well that if the people of the village get to him first, he will be treated badly. So he *runs* – an indignity to which an eastern father would not under any circumstances subject himself. He runs, with the family retainers following him. And to *their total shock* they see the old man hugging and embracing his returning son and through tears welcoming him home! This is not the way things are meant to be! No father, especially one who has been so flagrantly humiliated, would – or should – behave like that! And just in case there is any possibility of his actions being misread, he turns to them and says, 'what are you gawping at? Go and run a bath . . . bring the best robe, a ring, and then start preparing a banquet. We're going to celebrate tonight!' *That* is the moment when the son repents. The moment of unreserved welcome, unconditional, abundant grace. That is the moment when he stops thinking about how he can earn his way back into favour

. . . the moment when he is changed forever by his father's self-emptying, reconciling love. And, says Bailey, he empties himself again when the elder son, blazing with anger and resentment, returns from the field *and refuses to go into the banquet.* Father *goes out to meet him* pleading with him to come home and be reconciled to his brother – 'who was lost and is found; was dead and is alive again.'

In Wesley's extraordinary poem, 'Wrestling Jacob', the two stories from Genesis 32 and Luke 15 are fused. The first six verses ask the agonized question, 'Who are you? What is your name?' The other six all end with the affirmation, 'Your nature and your name is *Love*'.

This is the gospel within the gospels. What Wesley called 'prevenient grace' . . . the grace that goes *before* repentance. I am writing these lines in St Deniol's, the Gladstone Library at Hawarden near Chester. This morning at the Eucharist, the priest pronounced forgiveness *before* the prayer of confession, because, he said, 'God's gracious offer of pardon comes *before* our penitence. More than that, it is this incredible love which *leads us* to true penitence – the changing of our hearts.' This is what Geoff meant. This is why he believed Rembrandt was wrong. This is what he had discovered in his own experience; it was why it mattered so much to him. Here is the nature of God! Believe it! The very heart of the gospel. The best of all good news.

Learning how to die

When Alec Vidler and Malcolm Muggeridge travelled through Ireland in the 1970s they met an old woman sitting outside her cottage in a rural village. During their conversation the woman said that she was learning how to die. In a sense, the whole of our life is a preparation for death; in those times of leaving behind; the 'little deaths', prefiguring the moment of transition from mortal life into another country, a different climate, the life of eternity. He had spoken of receiving his illness as a gift. Now he was not just learning, but *teaching us* how to die with cheerfulness and courage. He became gradually weaker but was mercifully free from pain. As death approached on 4th January, we commended him to God with the family around him, 'in sure and certain hope of resurrection'. His barely audible amen was the last word he uttered.

Homecoming: anticipating the feast

Geoff had prepared his funeral with meticulous care. He had chosen hymns and readings and suggested how members of his family might be involved. He had asked for the reading of Psalm 8 at the thanksgiving service, to reflect how, in his latter years, he had come to appreciate more fully the wonders of modern science through the Darwin Society and stunning TV programmes, and how these amazing discoveries are transforming our lives and the world. For him they were signs of God's activity, not to be feared but welcomed and celebrated.

Heavy snow had fallen during the days prior to the funeral and it was feared that this might create travel problems for those coming from a distance. Thankfully there were no significant falls on 25th January, and the church was full for the service of thanksgiving with friends representing every phase of Geoff's ministry, joined by local Methodists, friends from other churches in the city and the Lichfield community. We sang 'Born in the Night'; Margaret read the gospel and Caroline led prayers; the Lichfield Cathedral singers sang 'Tomorrow shall be my dancing day'; and we concluded with Charles Wesley's great hymn, celebrating the love of God in Christ by which we are changed and made whole. It was a worthy tribute. Earlier at the crematorium service of commendation and committal, after Barbara and Colin had read the narratives of Jacob and the

Prodigal, Donald Eadie spoke movingly of Geoff the master storyteller and how he had found in those stories deep clues to the meaning of his own journey; how in baptism they define and transform our humanity.

> *For you* Christ came into the world. *For you* he lived and showed God's love, suffered and died . . . triumphed over death. *For you* he prays. *All this for you* before you could know anything of it. In your Baptism the word of Scripture is fulfilled:
> *We love because he first loved us.*

Donald showed us another Rembrandt work, an unfinished sketch which Geoff had shared with him and other close friends . . . a sketch which is almost certainly a depiction of the encounter of Simon Peter and Jesus on a Galilean beach after the resurrection. The disciple-fisherman is splashing through the waves towards the shore, following a fruitless night on the lake, and is brought up short by the charcoal fire as Jesus prepares breakfast for his tired, dispirited followers . . . he is remembering that other charcoal fire in a hostile place where he disowned his Friend three times with vehement curses . . . yet no confession is required, no absolution given, simply the invitation, 'come, eat breakfast'. And later the trusting and entrusting: 'I still love you . . . still believe in you; feed my sheep . . . follow me.' 'Perhaps all these stories,' suggested Donald, 'belong within the story of welcome and homecoming, the story of grace which Geoff loved to tell. He taught us to anticipate the feast. The last words that he whispered to me over the phone were, "all I can say is, Thanks be to God!" In our turn all we can say is the same, "Thanks be to God!"'

Just after Christmas in the week before he died, I visited Geoff and he asked me to read the prologue to John's gospel. I had reached, 'the Word became a human being and lived among us; and we saw his glory . . . from his abundance we have received grace upon grace . . .' I stopped, because I thought he had gone to sleep. By now he was sleeping most of the time. Then he opened his eyes, looked at me, smiled and said:

'Bloody marvellous!'

Indeed it is! Alleluia!

_____

All shall be well and all manner of thing shall be well and all shall be well.   (Julian of Norwich)

EPILOGUE
'MORE THAN . . .'
Donald Eadie

This book began within a grieving process that is being transformed through gratitude. It is more than a gift of memories for those who knew Geoffrey Ainger, much more than the story of a great storyteller. The book reclaims the deep places of transition within the life of the world, the glories and fragility of our own humanity as the terrain within which God's story weaves in mysterious, subterraneous ways. Geoff was more than a wrestling and wounded Jacob, he was both a herald and liberator into the new dawn. When his life-long friend, Norwyn Denny, suffered desperate anguish following an aneurism, Norwyn likened it to his descent into hell. Geoff wrote to him, including a quotation 'and he made of the abyss, a road'. Norwyn wrote later of his discovery that the road through the abyss leads to God. 'It confirmed for me the belief that "out of the depths I cry", is the point at which, when you are most in doubt and distress, presence and strength come.'

In his ageing years Geoff left us no book, there were a few poems, notes on Bible studies, retreats led, talks given. Warren has gathered the fragments and fashioned a glorious mosaic and more. He has researched the context of Geoff's life, provided continuity within what some may think of as a broken story, illumined his narrative with those primal Biblical stories in which Geoff found meaning and hope within our humanity. Warren shared Geoff's rich explorations, his relish in life during those later years, became his close friend and while Geoff was living with cancer Warren was both his companion and soul friend as he turned toward death.

My first encounter with Geoff was in the summer of 1968 during the World Council of Churches Assembly in Uppsala. One evening my wife's university friends invited into their home a few exhausted delegates to relax and enjoy the flavours of Swedish hospitality. There came a moment when conversation turned into the idiosyncrasies of religious broadcasting and, spontaneously, Geoff and Pauline Webb broke into a brilliant parody of a typical BBC programme. Their combined knowledge, their playfulness, insight and wit entertained us into the night bringing us into tears of laughter. It was as a foretaste, a feast in friendship.

Kerstin and I met Geoff again prior to our joining him in the Ecumenical Group Ministry and congregation in Notting Hill in 1972. On our arrival, we learned that Geoff had experienced a breakdown of health and also of marriage. This was a complex bereavement for both the congregation and colleagues. It was a shock for us also. Geoff entered the shadows.

The pilgrimage Geoff entered was more than a torrid wasteland, he 'lost his simplicity' and became 'a survivor washed up on the Rock of Ages' and much more. He discovered in the words of Edwin Muir's splendid little poem 'The Good Man in Hell' a new vocation, '. . . to kindle a little hope in hopeless hell and sow among the damned doubts of damnation.'

We met again in our retirement. When Barbara and Geoff moved to Lichfield in 1998, Ellen and Norwyn Denny were in Redditch, and we were in Birmingham. We shared meals together, found joy in each other, shared our explorations, commended reading, confessed our outrage at political obscenities. Always we laughed and laughed. Barbara and Geoff became our friends.

Norwyn, Geoff and I began to share our writings, engaging in correspondence. We exchanged jokes through the most draining of times, physical and emotional. Geoff wrote once of laughter,

> ... in the sharing of your experience of adversity, you become aware from time to time, not of a whistle, but of an echo of a primal music 'when all the morning stars sang together ...' Isn't it amazing that the biblical witness to such a fundamental, though hidden harmony should be by someone in the dark grip of affliction? You belong to that precious company of rumour-mongers whose mixture of stammering, silence and laughter bears witness to the glad strangeness of the gospel.'

Who writes and posts such letters now?

In September 2012 Geoff asked for 'a summit meeting', a confidential conversation. It is not for me to share the content of that long conversation. He invited me to do 'the tricky bit' at the crematorium with his family and close friends present, the 'handing over' into God. Warren had accepted the invitation to lead the Service of Thanksgiving. On that same Friday afternoon Geoff returned to the writing of Karl Barth, God's 'word' to us in our weakness, wickedness, marginalisation, flawedness, 'Yes, you are loved to the uttermost in the cross of Jesus. Yes and Amen.'

APPENDIX ONE

Bible Study: 'To give us fresh eyes'
Reflections on Faithful Imagination

This Bible Study over five sessions was held in Geoff and Barbara's home, Curborough Road, Lichfield, February–March 2007. It was inspired by Simon Schama's BBC TV series, 'The Power of Art', which was later issued as a book.

1 Field of vision and sharp focus

I suffer from glaucoma and before my driving licence can be renewed I have to undergo two tests. One is to read a car number plate at a specified distance; the other is to demonstrate that my peripheral vision is still good. To drive safely, it is necessary to bring into sharp focus what is in front of my eyes and also to have sufficiently broad vision to enable me to navigate my vehicle in traffic.

Simon Schama, the historian, in his recent brilliant TV series on the power of art, writes:

> It was a commonplace that art, both traditional and modern, should *give us fresh eyes* and enable us to see the ordinary as extraordinary.

> In the 1930s and 1940s, as in our own time, mass murder became ordinary, or so it would seem from newsprint and film. The work of art, Picasso came to believe, was to resist the

assumption that this was the way the world was and would ever be. He homed in on a small market town near Bilbao on a Monday afternoon in 1937 at 4.00 pm, when German bombers in support of General Franco had killed some 1,600 people and wounded many more. The name of the town was GUERNICA. Something vast was creeping across Europe, but to indicate what he had seen he focussed attention on this one incident.

As a teacher of English in London at a college of further education, I was trying to help students with descriptive writing: 'In one paragraph, describe ME!' was the challenge. One student described the ticket collector on the Tube - and it was just his hands which she remembered. The Zoom lens and the wide-angled shot.

But do we read THE BIBLE with tired eyes? We see the text, but it is sometimes so familiar or so obscure that we fail to recognize its essential truth.

Look at the Book of **Job.** Most of it is in verse that is from chapter 3 verse 1 to chapter 42 verse 6. This is, if you like, the zoom lens, which gives us a sharp focus on Job's suffering. *But look at the wide-angle lens which leads us into the drama.*

Read: **Job 1:1–5.**   (Historical setting)

Read: **Job 1:6–12.**   (Basic question of the drama is in verse 9)

Read: **Job 1:13–22.**   (The gathering challenge to Job's faith)

Read: **Job 2:1–23.**   (The intensified challenge)

THEN – the ZOOM LENS takes over!

Read: **Job 2:9–10.** (His wife's question and counter-question)

Read: **Job 4:7-21.** Eliphaz looks at Job through the 'eyes of faith', through a lens that would make God just by making Job guilty. If suffering comes you must deserve it!

See **John 9.** Who sinned? This blind man or his parents? That's where we must look for meaning. But from the heart of his particular calamity Job raises an agonized question about the *meaning of anything.*

Read: **Job 9:13-24.**

Read: **Job 23:1-10.** Faith in the fog! If I could find him I would get a hearing. I would be acquitted. Job in the terrible confinement of his affliction refuses to see his predicament with the *tired eyes* of conventional religion of resigned unbelief. If there is no God then there *is* no problem of evil and suffering. If you do believe there is a real problem when trouble comes.

Arthur Koestler, captured by the Fascists during the Spanish Civil War, describes being put into solitary confinement. Shut in a tiny cell, he decides to 'set out on a voyage of discovery around my new domain - eight feet by ten. The heavy metal door had no handle on the inside, and in it was a spy-hole, in which from time to time an eye would appear. It was an eye without a man attached.' Note the sharp focus of the detail and also the 'wide-angle' words, which makes you collide with the experience of his helpless confinement. ('Voyage of discovery ... my new domain.' The eye 'without a man attached', eloquently impersonal. Back to the hands of the ticket-collector!)

Read: **John 13:1-1.** Washing the disciples' feet. The *zoom lens* brings into focus Jesus the shoe shine boy. Verse 3's wide-angle shot puts the act into its proper context.
NB: John Bunyan's opening of *Pilgrim's Progress* (1675).

Read the opening paragraph: 'As I walked through the wilderness of this world I lighted upon a certain place where a den ...'

He was literally imprisoned by conventional religion. But from the cell he fashions a whole world of faith and imagination. We are all imprisoned in everyday life; if we can see with fresh eyes we are enabled to get up and walk. *God has faith in us.*

'I cannot tell ... but this I know ...'

EPWORTH REVIEW, APRIL 2005: words of MARION CRAWFORD, a METHODIST MINISTER:

'There are certain events in our lives which are totally life-changing and the birth of our second daughter was one such event, although I didn't realise at the time how much she would influence my faith, theology and ministry.' The little girl had Down's syndrome. 'With Clare's birth *I began a journey of DISCOVERY.'* They visited Lourdes and went to the grotto of the Virgin Mary. *'I SAW FOR THE FIRST TIME Mary as the mother of a son who was broken and on the cross disabled. Clare is created in the image of God.'* When the walls were falling in on her, something new began.

But the gift of 'seeing with fresh eyes' does not always or necessarily come in the 'twinkling of an eye'.

Read: **Mark 8:22–26.** 'I see men as trees walking ...'

Read: **Mark 8:27–33.** 'You are the Christ.' True ... but ... Peter rejects the suffering road. *He does not in fact see clearly until after the resurrection.*

John zooms in on Jesus' deadness.

Read: **John 19:31–34.** Note the tiny details about the body. Christ shares our essential human-ness in life and death. BUT, before delivering his gospel to the churches, the evangelist pulls back and, like the writer of Job, uses the *wide-angle lens*, setting his story in the context of its fundamental meaning. Read **John 1:1–14.**

2 Healing our diseased vision

What prevents us from seeing properly?

The problem may be short-sightedness. Although they couldn't read a sentence without glasses, they can see the details of a cricket scoreboard from a few hundred yards distance. Some have the opposite problem. This serves to illustrate the truth that eyesight deteriorates, or it becomes diseased, defective ... we may need to change our spectacles more often, or maybe an operation is required to cure a cataract, etc. Some eye diseases are as yet incurable. So we consider in this session, the healing, making whole of our inner sight. The story of the blind man whose sight was restored by Jesus, said that initially he saw 'men as trees walking' – an indication that healing is sometimes if not always, a gradual process.

What are the symptoms of defective vision?

1　The *wood–trees syndrome*: 'he can't see the wood for the trees', 'she can't see beyond her nose-end'. This is a fault in the long-distance vision.

2　*One-dimensional vision*: black and white, flat screen, no depth. 'You're imagining things.' Spielberg, the ultimate image man, says that the imagination needs to be educated. Our generation needs desperately to re-discover the power of *word* without which the image is incomplete.

3　*Distorted vision*: lens out of focus, like looking at yourself in a crazy mirror.

Let's start with latter point. Read: **Acts 9:1–19.** Saul's inner sight is distorted. He is on a mission of hate-fuelled destruction. His vision of God and his inner self is focussed on this terrible blood-lust. Where does this come from? Christ meets him on the outskirts of the city; he is *blinded* and carried into the city, helpless, to Straight Street. Ananias one of the unsung heroes of the early church becomes the human bridge over which Saul crosses into the Christian community. Notice the moment when 'the scales fell from his eyes', the moment when the distorting lens through which he had seen life began to be healed. 'Brother Saul'; a moment of total acceptance and forgiveness, healing the blindness of fear, hate and prejudice. John Masefield in the 'Everlasting mercy'. Once I was blind – now I see. Christ has double vision!

Then there is the 'one-dimensional' distortion. Read **Acts 10:1–6, 34–48.** Remember 3-D? Like many people, Peter's eyesight was one-dimensional. If A is true, B must be untrue. Either one thing or the other. None so blind as those who will not see. **Acts 10** is about the conversion of Peter to God's multi-dimensional way of seeing. The Spirit opens our eyes to the kaleidoscopic nature of God's vision. Read **2 Cor. 5:16–18, Galatians 3:26–28, Ephesians 3:8–11** (Greek: *polupoikilos* – multi-coloured).

The 'wood–trees syndrome' can be illustrated by two Old Testament passages. Read **2 Kings 6:8–20.** A thriller. How can we possibly get out of this hole? What is it that the young man with his myopic vision has failed to see? 'Lo, to faith's *enlightened sight.*'

Life is not a long day's journey into night. Healing our distance seeing is about the re-birth of *hope.* Read **Jeremiah 32:6–15.** 'From the depths of the Good Friday experience of destruction and the certainty of a Saturday of exile comes this Sunday word' (Brueggemann). In the midst of death and destruction the seer John envisions a new heaven and a new earth. Bobby Kennedy said: *Some people see things that are, and ask, why? I see things that never were and ask, why not?* The dreadful scenarios around global warming are not science fiction, but this is not the only or the greatest reality. Landing at Heathrow in March hits you with the harsh reality of English winter. But above the cloud and rain, is the greater reality of blue sky and sun. Sometimes we have to wait at the gap between tears and laughter believing that 'joy comes in the morning'. We need a long pause when reading **Philippians 2: 5-11** before 'therefore'.

So, how does God heal, make whole our blinded sight?

A major clue is in the experience of another prophet, Ezekiel. Read **Chapter 3: 12-15.** 'I sat where they sat.' He saw life, reality through the lens of *their* experience. He saw the wretched truth of what it means to be a refugee/exile/asylum seeker. This is the gift of a sympathetic imagination that comes when we begin to live, walk, in someone else's shoes. Attending to the inner meaning of a painting means attending to the context of the painter's experience. E.g. Rembrandt and the Prodigal son.

Read: **John Hull's story of what it means to be blind** (*Epworth Review*, January 2007, pp. 69-79).

This is the truth of *Costly Incarnation.* God inhabits our skin, experiences our humanity. To pray with blind Bartimaeus, 'Lord I want my sight back', is a costly prayer. Life can never be the same again. Christian vision is subversive. Seamus Heaney describing the boldness of Nazhezda Mandelstam in the Romanian revolution says:

> Suddenly she became a *guerilla of the imagination* ... from then on she was like a hunted priest in penal times, travelling dangerously with the altar-stone of the forbidden

faith, disposing the manuscripts for safe keeping among the secret adherents. And inevitably having considered herself a guardian *she was destined to become a witness.*

3 Seeing differently: (In)sight as protest

How would you define a *Protestant*? What does the word *Protest* mean?

The word derives from the Latin *pro-testare,* to 'testify in favour of'.

Think of the way in which the word is sometimes used: Protests ... demonstrations ... anti-apartheid ... anti-abortion ... anti-Iraq war. Protests are usually seen as being against something. A protest is another way of saying 'No'.

But behind the 'antis' lurks *affirmation.* 'Man shall not live by disinfection alone'!

We can't understand the *Protestant Reformation* if we believe that Martin Luther was simply driven by the word 'No'. He testified to the unconditional grace of God in Christ, and attacked church doctrine and practice that covered up or denied God's fundamental *YES!* To humanity.

We look at Pablo Picasso's painting of Guernica. It is the work of a 20th-century 'protestant'. During the Spanish Civil War, on Monday 26th April 1937, in the market town of Guernica, fifteen miles from Bilbao, it was market day. At about 4.00 pm fascist bombers raided the town for three hours and set fire to it. 1,645 people were killed and thousands injured. How did the perpetrators of this atrocity see it?

Lt. Colonel Von Richtoven, commander of the Condor Legion in Spain reported: *Guernica literally levelled to the ground: bomb craters in the streets ... simply terrific ... perfect conditions for a great victory.*

Walter Brueggemann, the great Old Testament scholar, wants to look at what 'the meeting of church liturgy and gospel preaching is all about. *It is a place where people come to receive new materials, or old materials freshly voiced, that will feed, fund, nourish and authorize a COUNTER-IMAGINATION OF THE WORLD.'*

What does he mean by that? Let's look at some examples from the Bible

Mark 14:51. This only occurs in Mark. Is this a 'cartoon' in the corner of the arrest scene? What does the cloak represent?

Genesis 37:31-34. Joseph's bloodstained coat. Full stop.

Genesis 39:11-12. Potiphar's wife ... left with his coat!

John 20:6-7. 'Linen cloths' in sepulchre.

Back to *Guernica. Look carefully at the painting. What do you SEE? The 'seeing' is not 'objective' or detached.* Look at the electric light in the painting ('eye' with man attached). Look at the candle, so vulnerable. Here is *involved art.*

What is the perspective of the *victims?* The painting is in a museum near Alosha station in Madrid where three bombs killed many on 11/3/2004. Read **Psalm 2.** 'Golgotha ... were you there when they crucified my Lord?'

Notice too that Guernica is painted as a *night attack* ... but it was a *daylight raid.* Earl Grey said in 1914, *'The lights are going out all over Europe.'* The Jew Elie Wiesel called his book on Auschwitz, simply *Night.*

Read **John 13:30** and **Mark 15:33**.

Look at the *Tearing apart* in the painting. In AD 70 the Romans tore down the veil of the Holy of Holies, and found nothing. Read **Hebrews 10:19-20**.

Picasso's painting arrived in London on 29/9/38, the day Chamberlain signed the Munich agreement: 'I have here on this piece of paper, the signature of Herr Hitler ...'

Read **Ezekiel 37:1-14**. The Valley of Dry Bones. A classical example of protestant proclamation ... of seeing differently ... of talk of *RESURRECTION*. The eyes that glimpse Promise.

Read **Revelation 5: 1-14**. They sang a new song (v.9). Not from the usual hymnsheet!

On 13th February, in Hinde Street, London, Canon Lucy Winkett, Precentor at St. Paul's Cathedral, spoke on Charles Wesley and entitled her lecture *'Singing as an act of resistance'*.

Here, we are suggesting that to be able to see differently to put on 'protestant' spectacles contributes not only to the healing of our vision, which we considered last time, but also to the healing of our world. To quote Simon Schama:

> This is what all great art should do: crash into our lazy routines. Guernica fights the truly deadly habit, a sickness of our own time as of his. Of taking violent evil in our stride, of yawning at the video-massacre; seen it all before; go away; don't spoil the fun of art. Guernica wasn't made for fun. It was meant to rip away the scar tissue, rob us of our sleep. It did. So in every way that mattered, Picasso had won, art had won, humanity had won.

That's resurrection talk!

4 Sepia light: Seeing as remembering

There is a film about a young man who on a particular day and for no apparent reason suffered a rare total memory loss; like a computer crash; files irretrievably lost.

The film went on to describe the terrifying, painstaking, lengthy process of re-discovering his identity. Who we are, both individually and corporately is bound up with remembering ... memory gives us roots, identity and therefore hope. Going through old photo albums can generate a whole range of emotions from pleasure to pain. Memory can be fickle. Two people from the same family may see an identical photograph of a long dead relative quite differently. Subsequent events, attitudes, etc., colour the recall. Sometimes the lens through which we view the past needs to be cleaned. Some memories need to be healed.

(a) Personal remembering: California dreamin'

Nostalgia: you may know the song *California Dreamin'*, which expresses not just the rootlessness and nostalgia of 1960's American youth, but evokes an older American dream ... the longing of poor travellers and would-be settlers for California. A. E. Housman's poem, 'Bredon Hill', captures the same poignant longing. But was the past always what our mental and sepia photographs tell us it was? Or is there some process of selection going on?

Remembering can *renew hope*. Read **Psalm 42/43**. The Psalmist uses past experience to address his depression. Remembering can also *fortify us in present struggles*.

Read **1 Samuel 21:8-9**. David, with his back to the wall and uncertain of the future, remembers a time when he won a great victory. The young ex-offender who carried a photograph of his mentor always with him: 'It helps me to keep straight.'

But, in **Psalm 137** we see how remembering, in a place of disorientation can produce *bitterness and hatred.* Remember Housman's 'land of *lost content'.* This experience is perpetuated in our own time. Poland 1942. How we deal with memories of this kind is one of the acid tests of the reality of our faith. We can become trapped in longing for this lost territory. Yet our past is uniquely ours, and therefore uniquely precious. Where we've come from, who we are and what direction we need to take. But we can never go back to the past – only forward. Notice how true this is of Biblical heroes. We must beware of seeing ourselves and others only through the spectacles of yesterday. Notice how Jesus *redeems* Peter's remembering.

Read **Luke 22:54-62** and **John 21:9-17.** Consider how the stored photograph of his denial would have haunted and disabled Peter for the rest of his life. The remembering is radically altered by grace.

(b) Communal Remembering: Rule Britannia!

We all have memories, photographs that are shared with millions of other people. Patriotism. What emotions, rememberings are stirred in you by pictures of the Union Jack ... or the singing of a national anthem? Turner's painting of Trafalgar. The tragedy of the de-valuing of history in schools ... But we have to recognize that history is more often than not written by the winners. We have to be careful of the lens we use!

Read **Psalm 78:52-55.** What do photographs of our history tell us about who we are? In the Pentateuch we find the Mosaic writers using communal remembering to stress the obligations of justice. Read **Leviticus 19:33-34** and **Deuteronomy 15:12-15.**

Remembering of the tribe ... the need to record stories. Old people and the importance of their memories; giving depth and resonance to the present. Exiles should have the right to return but under what conditions? Cf. Palestine: what does the 'right to return' mean for Palestinians? The young Jewess, Dalia Landau, when visited by Bashir, and his brother, Palestinians who had been driven out of the house she now occupied in 1947 said: 'In that moment, I made room for the other side.' Looking at and taking account of the photographs of the other side. Seeing with fresh eyes.

(c) The Remembering of God: Have you forgotten us?

Read **Psalm 89:38-52**. This is a prime example of a strand of protest in the Old Testament that berates God for his apparent loss of memory. Have you forgotten us? Look at these photographs! See what we've come to! Don't you care? They call on God to *remember his covenant* ... and there are many passages which refer to God remembering his covenant and acting to save his people. Read: **Exodus 3:7-9; Isaiah 49:14-16; Psalm 98:3; Luke 1:72**.

(d) What is the significance of these snapshots of the past?

Story, past, identity. Some regimes try to erase communal memory, e.g. the Soviets re-writing their own history without reference to the dissidents. Read **John 16:4**. The Holy Spirit as 'remembrancer'. Jesus remembered. Brian Keenan: *My father became not just simply a memory but a real presence.*

Defining people, events over against the prevailing power. We are in exile; the prevailing culture is essentially idolatrous. Matthew's genealogy of Jesus is subversive.

Helps us to imagine and anticipate a new future. 'Future and past subsisting now' (C. Wesley). Read **Psalm 71**. Underpins the Eucharist. Not simply a "memorial"; it is *anamnesis* remembering, re-presenting ... at the heart of the church's self-awareness.

My father became not ... a memory but a *real presence*. We are held deep in the transforming memory of God, utterly loved by One in whom our past and future are forever present.

5. Fidelity, failure, hospitality, (in)sight.

The Bible is the lens through which we seek to bring our world into focus and, having seen, to bear witness (pro-testare). Those who see most sharply and profoundly are often either the young or newly-arrived, or the old and experienced (e.g. Samuel, Simeon and Anna). It is as if our 'distance vision' is sharper than our 'near sight'. This is suggested in De Tocqueville's picture of 19th-century American society, 'the Emperor with no clothes'.

We begin with the Emmaus story, a classic example of people being given 'fresh eyes'; the ability to perceive what is profoundly true.

Read: Luke 24:13–35. We may compare this with other gospel records of blind people receiving their sight. Note especially v.31, 'their eyes were opened and they recognized him'.

But, what journey had they undertaken to reach their front door?

(a) *A journey beginning with FIDELITY*
Note verse 17, 'they stood still, looking sad'; and verse 31, 'we had hoped that he was the one to redeem Israel'. They were not detached from the fate of Jesus of Nazareth.

They had been involved in the enterprise. They didn't simply hold up their hands in horror and say, 'Shocking! What on earth is the world coming to?' (In verses 18–21, it appeared that the enterprise of Jesus and their enterprise had sunk without trace when he died on the cross.) This was also true of the other disciples. They followed because they *trusted him.* Before we look at their faith we must pay attention to their *faithfulness.*

Read **Mark 8:27–30.** Simon Peter is putting all his eggs in Jesus' basket! Imagine what that must have meant in 1st-century Palestine – to ask everything. Peter is prepared to be loyal though he doesn't see clearly. His eyes will only be fully opened by the cross and resurrection. For now he sees 'men as trees walking' **(Mark 8:22–26).**

Read **John 11:1–6.** Thomas is realistic. He sees the danger. The last time we were in Jerusalem they threatened to stone us, but 'let us go that we may die with him'. This is 'doubting' Thomas!

Read **Mark 14:26–31.** 'You will all abandon me,' evokes Peter's vehement protest, 'though all the others abandon you I will never let you down.'

Read **Luke 22:28–30.** 'You are the ones who have *continued with me in my trials.'* Not just the last week; his whole ministry had been a rocky road.

NB: Orthodoxy is 'believing the right things': orthopraxis is 'doing the right things'. For disciples, the latter comes first.

In the garden, Jesus pleads with them to 'watch with me'. Bonhoeffer said, 'In the 20th century, the characteristic form of discipleship is to stay awake with Christ in Gethsemane.'

Neville Ward in his book, *Five for Sorrow, Ten for Joy,*[19]

---

[19] J. Neville Ward, *Five for Sorrow, Ten for Joy*, Church Publishing Inc, 2005.

wrote, 'Only people who had known and loved him could say what "seeing him" means.'

(b) *FAILURE*

The Emmaus pair walked into the gathering gloom as members of a band of disciples, whose Messiah had failed, and who *at the critical moment had failed him.* We recall Napoleon's retreat from Moscow. This walk to Emmaus was *the retreat from Golgotha.*

At the heart of the story of the beginnings of Christianity lies the confession of the first disciples.

Read **Mark 14:43–50.** Note: we have the protective blanket of medieval Christianity, but Mark is brutally specific. Judas was *one of the Twelve.* There are critical moments of failure. It is not just the Jewish and Roman authorities who are responsible, but a member of the inner circle. Then they all fled. Presumably, if Jesus had said, 'come on lads, let's fight it out', they might have all died together in the ensuing melée, but that was not the way of this Messiah.

Read **Mark 14:66–72.** Detached theorists would not have got as far as the courtyard. But he had followed as far as he could.

G.K. Chesterton said: 'The man who makes a vow makes an appointment with himself at some distant time or place. The danger of it is that he should not keep that appointment.'

Peter is the Rock because he dared to make the vow, even though he failed. So we have St Peter's in Rome. He learned in his failure the meaning of grace and forgiveness.

(c) *HOSPITALITY*

Read **Luke 24:28–30.** If they hadn't asked him in *before they knew who he was* they would have remained un-seeing.

Read **Genesis 18:1-5**. Abraham and Sarah welcome three strangers. They could have turned them away, carried on living in the shadow of a full-stop. They seemed to have no future. It was the giving of hospitality which opened the way to the renewal of promise.

What had not been defeated in the hearts of these grieving disciples, was human kindness, generosity, expressed in hospitality to this stranger. That opened the door to the opening of their eyes.

APPENDIX TWO

Three songs and a poem

These songs are a small selection from a number which Geoff composed both at Notting Hill and at other times. The poem 'Is Horeb ever more remote?' was written in memory of his friend, the Rev. Brian Duckworth who died in 2003.

HOLY SPIRIT COME

ORPINGTON (5,5,8,5)

Geoffrey Ainger (1925–)
arranged Peter R. Burge (196–)

1 Holy Spirit come;
  Inspire our praying.
  That we may touch
    your life in God
  Beyond our saying.

2 Holy Spirit, come;
  Inform our knowing.
  That we may follow
    after truth
  Beyond our showing.

3 Holy Spirit come;
  Enrich our meeting.
  That we may others
    now include
  Beyond our greeting.

4 Holy Spirit, come;
  Direct our living.
  That we may share a
    daily grace
  Beyond our giving.

5 Holy Spirit, come;
  Comfort our sighing.
  That we may hope
    for life renewed
  Beyond our dying.

Geoffrey J. Ainger (1925–)

THERE IS NO BEGINNING TO GOD'S LOVE

Manningtree   *Geoffrey J. Ainger.*

1 There is no beginning
    to God's love
  as there can be no
    ending.
  This is the nature of the
    Lord
  this befriending.

2 There is a compassion
    in God's ways
  as with the shepherd
    tending.
  This is the practice of the
    Lord
  this defending.

3 There is an intention
    in God's care
  as with a craftsman
    mending.
  This is the purpose of the
    Lord
  this attending.

4 There is a revealing
    in God's gift
  as Christ comes lowly
    bending.
  This is the image of the
    Lord
  this descending.

Geoffrey J. Ainger.
Marking the 200 years celebration
2007-Methodist Church, Manningtree

S&B CAROLS

Geoffrey Ainger
and
Ian Calvert

A CRY IN THE NIGHT

arranged for

Unison Voices
(with Optional Descant)

and Piano (or Keyboards)

A CRY IN THE NIGHT

Becoming Human

102

IS HOREB EVER MORE REMOTE?
A poem for Brian Duckworth

Is Horeb ever more remote?
Has the blazing bush
which once became
the voice of God
burning with anger at injustice,
now become little more than
the quenched memory of God's people?

Are we still capable of fear in the
Presence of God
requiring of us a dangerous obedience
that seeks justice and compassion
before the saying of our prayers?

Do we still take off our shoes?

Thank God for those who have done
just that, who've understood that
grace is free but never cheap
and have stood in Pharaoh's presence
on behalf of those invisible to power.

Thank God for those who've glimpsed
the face of Christ who comes
not altogether as one unknown but as
healer of those in need,
sharing their necessity,
bearing the world's profound anxiety.

Thank God for the story of that
Second Eden
where streams shall flow through
the midst of the city with
open gates
and where the tree of life
sheds its leaves
for the healing of the nations.

Geoffrey Ainger

APPENDIX THREE

Final words

A sermon preached at the re-opening of Lichfield Methodist Church, 15th September 2012

I was about to apologize for having to sit down while I talk to you. But then I realized that there is a precedent.

He went up on the mountain and when he sat down his disciples came to him. And he opened his mouth and taught them, saying . . .!

First, I would like to add my words of congratulation and thanks to all of you who have been involved in the splendid transformation of this building. It is a delight.

It is a long time since I preached my first sermon. When I was nine years old my brother Peter and I thought it would be a good idea to conduct a 'do-it-yourself' service at our home in Norwich. We dragooned our luckless parents and grandparents to come into the dining room. Peter read the lesson – the parable of the Good Samaritan and I stood on a chair to preach on that text. Being good Methodists, we had, of course to take a collection . . . five old pennies! We were delighted to have such an amount and after the service we put our heads together as to what we might do with the money. In those days there were slot machines into which you could put two pence and get five Woodbine cigarettes in a little green packet. Two and a half each to be smoked in the coal shed at the bottom of the garden!

This ungodly plot was, however, foiled by mother who appeared with our family missionary box and insisted that the money should go towards the conversion of Africa.

I mention this tale of juvenile imagination and cupidity because the one thing we had got right was to focus on a story.

Why spend so much time, effort and money to transform this church as a place set apart for worship when we already have premises for meeting, for conversation and for all kinds of community activity? Because, at the heart of our open community, there is a particular story that is more than an echo of the tales we tell each other or hear on the News. It is the story of our humanity as touched by transcendence, challenged by a call to leave the known and secure and to risk responding to the call of the crucified Jesus.

As a young minister I attended a conference in Birmingham at which an American spoke very powerfully on the role of the ministry. 'It is the essential role of the minister,' he said, 'to be responsible for the story.' It is also the role of a Christian congregation within a multi-cultural and multi-faith society.

We have listened to a new version of Psalm 122 written by Rupert and Malcolm. This was a 'psalm of ascent', sung by Jewish pilgrims as they made their way into the highlands of Judea en route to the holy city of Jerusalem and the Temple.

Our world continues to be full of pilgrims: Hindus to the Ganges, Muslims to Mecca, Christians to Bethlehem, the devotees of rock and roll to Graceland, the home of Elvis. All are drawn by experience shaped by stories, stories which 'uncover life'. But they can only do that if our reading or telling of those stories gives priority to *the uncovering of the truth.*

Twenty-three years ago, 96 people were killed by being crushed to death at a football match at Hillsborough in Sheffield. This week a Report was published detailing who was responsible for such a tragedy. It only saw the light of day because a committee, largely consisting of the families of those who had died, stubbornly refused to be satisfied with official 'explanations' and the apportioning of responsibility.

During all that time the major organs of our State and of our culture had colluded in the lie that the misbehaviour of the fans, including those who had died, was the real cause of the disaster. This week, the Prime Minister stood up in the House of Commons to apologize on behalf of the Government for having failed to 'take responsibility for the story', for having failed over decades to pursue the truth. His apology was quickly followed by similar statements from the Football Association, the Emergency Services, the Police and the Press.

Now that Canon Pete Wilcox has gone from Lichfield to become Dean of Liverpool, we do perhaps feel a closer bond with that city and its people.

But all this raises questions for our own reading of the Bible and the practice of our faith.

We love to turn to Psalm 23, especially at weddings and funerals. 'The Lord is my shepherd' . . . that is where we get the expression 'pastoral care'. But should this be privatized, individualized? How often do we turn to that great prophet of the Exile, Ezekiel and to chapter 34?

> Son of man, prophesy against the shepherds of Israel . . .
> the weak you have not strengthened, the sick you have not
> healed, the crippled you have not bound up, the strayed
> you have not brought back, the lost you have not sought
> . . . I myself will be the shepherd of my sheep.

'I am the Good Shepherd,' Jesus said.

But it is not only secular authorities who should find this story disturbing. In 1989, months before the Berlin Wall came down, on a visit to Leipzig in East Germany I met an impressive young Lutheran scholar who has since become Professor of

New Testament at a university on the Baltic. When Barbara and I went to visit him and his family in their new home he showed me into his study. On his bookshelves there was a whole series of commentaries on St Luke's Gospel. It was, apparently, the custom for each newly appointed incumbent to write his own to add to the tradition. My friend picked out one particular edition which had been published in the 1940s under the Nazi regime. There, the professor had 'cleaned up' the gospel story, making the Jews responsible for crucifying Jesus and depicting that good Aryan Pontius Pilate as being innocent of any wrongdoing. The trouble was, of course, that the professor concerned read the text with eyes focussed on the back story of anti-semitic racism that led to his failure to be responsible for the story as told by St Luke.

In Luke chapter 4 we read of Jesus' first sermon in his home town synagogue at Nazareth. He took as his text those wonderful words from Isaiah 61, 'The Spirit of the Lord is upon me, because he has anointed me to preach good news to the poor . . .'

His words were received with acclaim! But then he went on to say that the great prophet Elijah's life was saved by the generosity of a widow who was a foreigner! And there were many lepers in Israel in the time of Elisha the prophet, 'and none of them were cleansed, but only Naaman the Syrian'. Jesus had been responsible for the story in a way they found quite shocking . . . and they would have lynched him.

When we pay attention to the gospel stories it becomes clear that Jesus was often uneasy in church (synagogue). We get hints of this from the story of the healing of the man with the withered hand in Mark 3, to the cleansing of the Temple in Mark 11. When, in Mark 13, the disciples, admiring the gleaming new buildings of Herod's Temple, said 'Look Teacher, what

wonderful stones and what wonderful buildings!' Jesus promptly
warns of their imminent destruction.

In the third chapter of the book of Revelation, the writer
depicts the risen Christ as being mightily unimpressed by a
'successful' church:

> You say I am rich, I have prospered, and I need nothing;
> not knowing that you are wretched, pitiable, poor, blind
> and naked.

'Behold I stand at the door and knock . . .' That is not the
heart's door. It is the church door. The church is full, the liturgy
is impressive, the programme is the envy of many. But Christ is
shut out. The Jesus of the Gospels has become a stranger.

Martin Luther said that when the Church is true to the
Gospel it is 'semper penitens' – always penitent. By that he did
not mean it consisted of 'miserable sinners', pre-occupied with
what Dietrich Bonhoeffer called 'a priestly sniffing around for
sins'. He remembered that in the Old Testament when God
calls on his People to repent, he uses the word, 'Return, O
Israel' . . . Come home!

Lastly we need to remember that this story for which we are
responsible is essentially a *story of hope.* In this service we have
read Genesis 28, the story of Jacob's ladder, a dream sequence
linking earth to heaven. The slaves in the American plantations
under the brutal cul-de-sac of exploitation, used to sing the
spiritual, 'We are climbing Jacob's ladder . . . every rung goes
higher . . . soldiers of the Cross!'

In Revelation 21 we read:

> Then I saw a new heaven and a new earth . . . and I saw
> the holy city, New Jerusalem, coming down out of heaven
> from God . . . (v. 22), and I saw no temple in the city, for
> its temple is the Lord God and the Lamb.

This morning I read a book review in the *Guardian* by Richard Holloway who used to be bishop of Edinburgh. He says of the author, 'He is also good at describing what it feels to sit silently in front of the resonant absence and feel beckoned beyond it.' Here we would be responsible for the story of the God-forsaken, dying Jesus and of the apparently plundered tomb on Easter morning. It is a story in which God is neither simply present nor simply absent. We come, hoping to feel beckoned, invited, welcomed by the mystery of grace.

APPENDIX FOUR

IN the sleeve on the inside back cover there is an accompanying CD containing a small selection of sermons from Geoff's ministry in Orpington 1984–1992.

i	*Evangelism.*	Morning of 1st July 1990
ii	*Baptism.*	Morning of 28th October 1990
iii	*Sienna and Colchester*	Morning of 6th October 1991
iv	*Vision and Imagination*	Morning of 17th May 1992
v	*Amen!*	Morning of 7th July 1992

All these sermons were preached at Orpington Methodist Church. *Amen* (v) was Geoff's last sermon before retirement.